A CHRISTIAN ETHIC
for the
MODERN CHURCH

DAVID GARCIA

LUCIDBOOKS

A Christian Ethic for the Modern Church
Copyright © 2022 by David Garcia

Published by Lucid Books in Houston, TX
www.LucidBooks.com

All rights reserved. No part of this publication may be reproduced, stored in a retrieval system, or transmitted in any form by any means, electronic, mechanical, photocopy, recording, or otherwise, without the prior permission of the publisher, except as provided for by USA copyright law.

Scripture quotations marked (ESV) are taken from the ESV® Bible (The Holy Bible, English Standard Version®), copyright © 2001 by Crossway, a publishing ministry of Good News Publishers. Used by permission. All rights reserved.

Scripture quotations marked (KJV) are taken from the King James Version (KJV): King James Version, public domain.

ISBN: 978-1-63296-561-5
eISBN: 978-1-63296-562-2

Special Sales: Most Lucid Books titles are available in special quantity discounts. Custom imprinting or excerpting can also be done to fit special needs. Contact Lucid Books at Info@LucidBooks.com

For Tim
I hope I was a good friend to you.

TABLE OF CONTENTS

Preface vii

1. On the Kingdom of God 1
2. Prayer 15
3. On the Christian in the World 25
4. Creation Care and Stewardship 69
5. Christianity, the Political Apparatus, and the Media 75
6. On the Institution of Church in America 83
7. A Proposed Organizational Ethic Drawn from Several Sources 123
8. A Proposed Personal Ethic Drawn from Several Sources 147
9. The Agape Feast 173

Afterword 181
Acknowledgments 185
Notes 187
Recommended Reading 191
About the Author 191

PREFACE

A number of what may seem to be disparate factors coalesced into the decision to write this little book. One of the stranger ones was the discovery of a spoon from the 1933 Chicago World's Fair while out shopping for antiques. On the end of the spoon is a face in relief, crowned with a banner and eagle. On the banner are the words, "I WILL." The fair was titled, "A Century of Progress." Its motto was "Science finds. Industry applies. Man adapts." There are fascinating color videos of the event on the internet that are well worth the watch.

The organizers built a literal city on Northerly Island in Chicago, a paean to the promise of science, technology, and human innovation to usher in a new utopia. That it was staged amid the Great Depression is interesting in itself and perhaps provides us with some insights into our psyche and the reality of our human condition.

It was the "I WILL" that stuck with me, though. It is commonly agreed among Biblical scholars that the five statements in Isaiah chapter 14, verses 13-14 that begin with those same words can be attributed to the devil or Satan. In essence, the statements represented the attempt or desire of the devil to supplant God and his authority. In a similar vein, we read the Genesis account of the tower of Babel, where the people attempted to *reach heaven* through human effort and ingenuity apart from the presence and direction of God. Scripture has many examples.

As I studied the history of American culture, our nation, and our way of life, I began to see the extent to which this myth holds sway over us, how a narrative of innovation and self-sufficiency is so pervasive that it hinders our ability to understand our society and the challenges we are facing at this point in history. Indeed, many of our most exalted virtues as a people may be major contributors to the crises we face. I hope to explore the disparities between what we may call the American way of life and the imperatives of God to his people the Church.

A second painful difficulty became apparent. I have heard many stories of those "offended" by the Church. I also heard the repeated refrain of recovering alcoholics and addicts with whom I have often been in contact saying, "I just couldn't get sober in church. I just couldn't get this deal in church." Others have had mental illness or less glamorous sin problems, or they had perceived rejection because of their socioeconomic status. Many have despaired of the "church as a business" model and have either left the church institution, are immersed in the corporate model for one reason or another, or are unable to articulate the deep disconnect and so hang on in confused desperation. I have had these experiences, and I know others who have as well. We as a body lament those who have "fallen through the cracks." On and on it goes, this offense at the hands of the church establishment. So often I have gotten offended at the offended. My hackles were raised. I was jealous for the Church, but at some point, I had to ask myself if some of the problems lay with me, with

Preface

us. Leaving a wide berth for the belligerent and hateful, for those who are determined to be offended regardless, and for those tares God says will grow up with the wheat until the end (Mt 13), I still had to ask if something was wrong with how we are "doing" this thing we call Church. To me, even that line of questioning reveals a disconnect of our modern psyche from the intention of God.

I began to review my own experience, to observe the experiences of others, as well as the economic and political behavior of the institution. I considered the corporate nature of church structure, and the crisis of meaning the man or woman in the pew so often endures in confused and silent guilt. I considered the lives of individual Christians, so often nominal at best, and without significant spiritual formation. They have not had grafted into them the organic community, the deep inner well of spiritual maturity and joy available in Christ. They are not revolutionary members of the kingdom of God, and their lives are often indistinguishable from those of the rest of the world. Theirs is a spiritual poverty, keeping them bound to the anxieties and institutions of the age, made all the more tragic by the availability of such riches in Jesus. I am confronting the crisis of my own spiritual poverty.

I had to take a serious look at those "least of us" who so often fall through the cracks, as they say. I had to look at the cult of celebrity among Christian ministers, the isolation of a corporatized and utilitarian model of church, and those genuine and well-meaning ministers who languish in frustration when the institution as it is, hems them into a lonely and inorganic existence.

As I began to study history and to look at current events and the state of the Church here, a frightening picture began to emerge, that of an institution in the coldest sense that exists

A Christian Ethic for the Modern Church

for its own survival and not for the proliferation of a pure gospel and the good of the wider world. This is evidenced in the endemic spirit of mammon (the will to wealth, power, and affluence) that exists within the Church, the lack of organic community among many professing Christians, the commodified church service, and the appalling lack of concern among so many of us toward the created order, the bitter political rhetoric being exercised under the supposed auspices of Jesus Christ, the widespread lack of spiritual formation, and the unapproachable nature of church leaders in direct contradiction to 1 Pet 5:2.

We praise God at the outset for his revelation of Jesus Christ to humanity, for the goodness of the creation, and for the impact the Church universal has so often had on the human condition. Christianity has contributed much to the world in the areas of education, health care, scientific endeavor, the sanctity of life, human identity, the separation of church and state for the benefit of all, a distinctive and defined moral ethic and imperative, meaning, purpose, the imperative to justice, and an eschatological hope that also has a great deal of bearing on our daily reality. It is true that God is present in his Church everywhere and working in the lives of people.

It must be recognized, however, that the presence of all the good the Church has done does not mean that there are no serious problems that need to be addressed with the utmost urgency. History is also rife with examples of Church compromise with the spirit of the age, whether economic, political, social, or moral. Complicity with evil has and continues to plague the Church, often in surprising ways. Unfortunately, these alliances are devastating for the Church and the individual Christian. We will examine in

Preface

general some of the psychological frameworks under which we operate and discuss how they may be at odds with God's intention.

We will consider how to locate ourselves historically and culturally, so that we may be able to connect with the next generations of human beings in awareness of their realities, many of which include deep resentments toward those of us who have come before. I contend that we can do this with full internal consistency of orthodox belief, and with an abundance of grace and truth toward all human beings, but we must first set our own house in order.

One of the psychological dynamics we face is that we often cannot conceive of alternatives to the status quo, and frankly do not even perceive the need to do so. One example that illustrates this principle well is politics. It is either this or that, left or right. (Although other parties are developing in response to the perennial frustrations of our current political climate, I contend that the Church has many separate metrics to consider regarding political involvement.) We are inundated with a stream of alarmist rhetoric from our "news" outlets that keep us in a state of outrage and fear. We feel powerless. This leads to anger and hatred toward *those others, out there*. This is the beginning of a deliberately instilled dehumanization and paranoia that fuels human exploitation and social engineering. We turn to the state or to a paradigm of insular church politics to protect us from the bogey-men out there. For some, true freedom may begin as easily as unplugging from the 24-hour news cycle. Constant exposure to the programming of this world, even when it promotes a victim mentality to the Church, serves to conform us to this world. The love and example of Christ are one of exposure and vulnerability, teaching us that his people are by design a counter-culture who trust in a higher authority. Living in the true Church offers meaning and fulfillment such as the world cannot give.

As the Western Church has adopted, and arguably created, the corporate, utilitarian mode of doing business, she has entered into a self-defeating cycle of church development. When troubles arise, as they always do among people, our human innovation, informed by the only framework we know, leads us to fight and argue and go build another one. We trust that the right people and the right programs will give us success, that the problems that arise are the devil, or the cost of doing business, or the frailty of humanity, those clay vessels. All of these things can be true in a measure, but few of us have dug down to the fundamental problem, which is the structure itself, so often modeled after corporations, both in practice and in spirit.

The purpose of this short book is to engage the myths that we have, in our modern, affluent culture, labored under for many generations. It is to expose the emptiness of a mechanistic view of life and to discuss options for corporate and personal renewal at a fundamental level. It is to contemplate psychological reintegration and holism in the Christian context.

We will begin by learning what it truly means to be a Christian, a member of the Kingdom of God. The setting right of this particular fact alone will begin to alleviate many difficulties within the Christian community and will assist in beginning to repair our relationships with those outside the Church, where wounds and resentments often abound.

We will investigate prayer as *the* fundamental Christian action. We may find relief from the sense of powerlessness that accompanies our media-driven society and avoid the

Preface

error of misguided and extremist political action that has so terribly damaged our witness in this nation.

Moving on, we will see how the deliberate development of an innocent, deep, and simple spiritual ethic can breathe real life, hope, and healing into us. It can make us the agents of significant change in our world, and in the lives of others. It can alleviate many of our chronic stresses, restore to us a sense of meaning, and provide a coherent message of hope to a distracted and confused world.

We will end our time with a meditation on the heart, the nature, and the intention of God from which we may hopefully discern the *spirit* of the thing and not just the *letter*. It is my earnest intention to speak a word of deep healing in a positive tone through an open examination of our deeply entrenched psychological frameworks. I intend to articulate the griefs of the wounded, the offended, and the ostracized both within and without the walls of the Church. It is to articulate the loneliness of the minister at the top of the pyramid who understands his or her dilemma and to challenge those who have succumbed to the allurements of power.

In doing all of this, many statements may seem to be unfair generalizations. We will not extensively discuss the myriad contributions of the body of Christ to humanity. This is regrettable, but the intention is to drive us to the crisis point, and the fork in the road. It is the fight that many of us need to have lest we pass on into obscurity as far as the kingdom of God is concerned. There are realities many of us are unaware of or are in denial of, and it is incumbent upon the people of God to reckon with our existence for the sake of the gospel, our sanctification, and the suffering world we inhabit. The prayer is that we will all be willing and able to face hard truths and pass by with internal honesty those things which do not apply.

Where I have failed in these ideals and intentions, I ask for your mercy and forgiveness. I do not believe that I have in any way militated against the Scripture or true Orthodoxy. If I have, please forgive me. It would seem that the current distortions within the Western Church have done far more violence to Scripture, the purposes of God, and human beings than any unintentional misrepresentations in this work. Facing the truth and confronting our deeply ingrained worldviews can be a terrifying process. It threatens to undo us. It has me.

I pray that you will read this work in the spirit of Philippians 1:9-11, "And this I pray, that your love may abound yet more and more in knowledge and in all judgment; That you may approve things that are excellent; that you may be sincere and without offense till the day of Christ; Being filled with the fruits of righteousness, which are by Jesus Christ, unto the glory and praise of God."

David Garcia,
10 November 2020

1
ON THE KINGDOM OF GOD

"For we wrestle not against flesh and blood, but against principalities, against powers, against the rulers of the darkness of this world, against spiritual wickedness in high places" (Ephesians 6:12 KJV).

cf: John 18:36, Luke 18:1, Daniel 9-10, 2 Kings 6:17 (A prayer for us all!)

It is first necessary that we reorient our understanding of reality to be in line with God's, as expressed in Scripture. All that follows rides on this. Otherwise, our only option is to live life according to the frameworks of the world, which have so often led the Church universal into compromise, weakness, and corruption, as history has shown. It leads the individual Christian into the same, and often into a place of frustrating ineffectiveness.

When the Church has married the State, the culture, or the spirit of mammon, she becomes an instrument of them and loses her power, her Agape, her salt, and light. Jesus told us that we are the salt of the earth. "But if the salt loses its savor, how can it be made salty again?" See Mt 5:13. Further, he says that we are the light of the world. And still, further, we are instructed to avoid the unequal yoke, and be separate. See 2 Cor 6:14-18. There is to be a distinction between the Christian and this world, between the Church and the systems of this world. It is indeed true that we are sprinkled as salt throughout this world and all of its systems, and this is a stewardship fraught with difficulties, but we must examine the nature of our "saltiness" in this age and culture, which so easily gives way to the will to power.

The good news is that with a proper understanding of the kingdom of God, we may find the right kind of power and Agape where it may be lacking. We will find that as individuals and as the Body we can take meaningful action and bring about meaningful changes, although our metric for success must be distinguished from that of the world if we are to see clearly. We will consider ministry and activism as vital but incomplete facets of the all-encompassing narrative of God. In this understanding lies the potential for untold peace and healing from the modern church mindset which often exhausts and wounds Christian people in the name of ministry.

In addition to a renewal of understanding, we must confront the state of the Body of Christ in America, our history and our current state of affairs, and our complicity in the attitudes and actions of this age. We must understand and consider how we have been "doing church" for these several generations. It is worth arguing that we have as a people tended to build our church governments after the patterns of this world and not after the admonition of God who instructed his people, "Feed the flock of God which is among you, taking the oversight thereof, not by constraint, but willingly; not for filthy lucre, but of a ready mind; *Neither as being lords over God's heritage,* but being ensamples to the flock" (1 Peter 5:2-3, KJV, emphasis mine). Church government and the handling of money must undergo a fundamental psychological change. We cannot teach financial stewardship classes in Sunday school and plunge the laity into massive debt through endless building campaigns. We would do well to stop managing our churches like factories or big box stores and begin building communities of people who can live together, experience healing, and be mobilized down to the last parishioner, even if our church growth looks different. A foundational point to consider is the spiritual aspect of our unified reality. It is easy to disregard this truth because it is, in a significant way, unseen. But that is a grave error. We live in a physical body with physical senses. Our lives and our actions are mediated through physicality. We cannot avoid this, nor should we. Much has been written from ancient times until now concerning the material and the immaterial as it relates to life, behavior, worldview, and ethics. Philosophic and religious inquiry have often come up with various systems to assign different values to the physical and the spiritual, material and immaterial. While these may seem obscure and esoteric thoughts, the results of these philosophical systems affect us more than we know.

In the simplest terms, for example, it was once put forward in Greek thought that the immaterial was the "real," and that the physical was but a shadow of the real. There is the reality of a thing, and then there is the *instance* or the *accident* of a thing, which is what we see, touch, handle, etc. This view of reality led to a better than/worse than line of reasoning, with the immaterial seen as higher or better, and by default the material esteemed as less.

A Christian Ethic for the Modern Church

That material of course includes the created order, and our bodies, and the bodies of others. We began to see what is created as a thing we can use at our whim, a gross distortion of God's original charge to mankind in the garden. We were created in his image and given the mandate to be co-regents with God over his "very good" creation. Sin led humanity to distort this original charge into one of exploitation and domination in an ungodly sense. Over time this led to the worst of human and environmental abuses and wastefulness, cruelty, racism, slavery, unbridled capitalism, and disparity. And our history asserts that this has so often been with the consent of, or even at the behest of, what has been expressed in our Western world as the Church. The acknowledgment and understanding of the less savory elements of our history will allow us as Christians to locate ourselves to greater effect in our current cultural milieu, even where we have been unfairly blamed. We can reach the world far better as ambassadors in a constant spirit of repentance and reconciliation than we can through unaware transactional evangelism. Blessed are the poor in spirit.

Ironically, the opposite philosophical distortion has led to the very same abuses, with an emphasis on the rationalization of human exploitation. Despite the many wonders of human endeavor, when the physical has been exalted above measure, sinful humanity has taken the charge in the garden as a mandate to *improve* the creation, to build and innovate with it to its highest degree. This sounds commendable on the surface, however, the reality has not borne out. This is the rationale employed throughout history by the colonialists to kill and enslave those undeveloped *savages* the world over, destroy their cultures, and take their lands and resources. This is the seed of genocide and environmental devastation. And, since it is impossible to commit atrocities without some kind of justification, humanity has developed deep and abiding psychology of hatred, racism, and classism that is so deeply embedded in our culture that it is often unrecognizable.

McCarraher's, *Enchantments of Mammon* lays out an exhaustive, erudite, and bitter pill; a history of this disproportionate elevation and deification of the material order and the distortion of God's original mandate. Mankind is to exploit and "improve" the material without restraint. To do less is to deny God's charge, to deny his order to divinize ourselves, and recognize the divinity in the things he has made. Early in American history, there was an element of millennialist theology in this, as the Church thought it was their duty to usher in the new Zion, to bring the world to perfection, and thus inaugurate the return of Christ. It is worth considering what our true motivations are, and how much effort has gone into the psychological frameworks we have developed to support them. We might compare the current "Seven Mountain Mandate" with this line of thought.

As the pessimism of the Great Depression and the wars following made the likelihood of "perfecting" the creation feel less and less possible or probable, the development of the premillennialist theology arose. Since the world is beyond repair, God is going to snatch his elect away to paradise at any minute. Then *things will get really bad,* but God will judge the world during the great tribulation. This kind of thinking comes with its own damages and distortions. It is a hard sell for sure to the suffering and persecuted Church the world over for whom things often could not possibly get worse. Also, it gives us further justification to use and destroy the creation because *it's all going to burn anyway.* It fails to take into account God's overall eschatological plan to renew what he has made. It ignores or misses the fact that much of the Christian's reason for being in this broken world is that we might be conformed to the image of Christ in preparation for our marriage to him. It fails to understand the imperative of God to his people to be *stewards*. It fails to understand that Jesus is going to return to *this earth* and establish his kingdom, that a new heaven and earth are renewed heavens and a renewed earth where, indeed, evil will be judged and removed, and where all the ugliness executed by evil mankind and the devil will be undone. See Mt 13:41-42. God will judge the wicked; a good and righteous God could do no other. Last, the rapture mindset, if you will, gives misguided Christian people justification for ignoring the pressing needs of the *now*.

It can be difficult to reconcile the need for justice and action in this world with the eschatological, or future, promises of God for renewal. Throughout the course of this work, I intend to show how our sanctification and eschatological hope are bound up together with our imperative to share the gospel and take direct action to the ends of love, justice, and care of the creation. I hope to construct a holistic psychological framework in which matter and spirit, present needs and future glory, are bound up and understood as a unity of thought, action, and purpose. This can bring healing to the divided American psyche. *How we are* in the world as individuals and as a Body directly impacts how we are perceived and what we can accomplish as concerns the proliferation of the gospel. It would do the Church a world of good right now to repair her witness to this current generation.

At any rate, as sinful mankind set about to perfect and utilize the created order, we embarked on a campaign of devastation that has not ceased. If we are willing to look, we can easily see the fruits of this: the driving of the populace to urban centers and destruction of small farms and communities, economic oppression, monopoly, exploitation, the genocide, atrocities, and continuing injustices committed against the Native Americans, the Industrial Revolution, the slavery we have only exported to the third world, the unbridled consumption and debt, the excess of living, the distraction and misplaced hope accelerated by the technological revolution, the refusal of God's people to live simply and within their means to the hurt of self and gospel, the denuding of the continent and overuse of its resources, the gross loss of species and habitat, and the indifference and hostility with which we treat our environment, God's property. As James' epistle warns the rich, "You have lived in pleasure upon the earth and been wanton [wasteful, merciless, inhumane, extravagant, undisciplined, sensual] . . . you have nourished your hearts as in a day of slaughter" (James 5:5-6, KJV).

Likewise, diminishing the value, and the presence and signature of God in his creation is the psychological basis of shame and utilitarianism. It is the reason we cannot observe God's Sabbath and enjoy what is made. It is the dissolution of beauty and art, the loss of joy in all its forms, the reason we have turned from the *imago Dei* inherent in craftsmanship to the psychological division of mass industrial production. It is the reason we wantonly destroy our ecosystems for economic gain. It is the basis of the rigid and shame-based morality that so many people have often suffered under, unable to find joy in life, marriage, rest, nature, or art. It is the very miserable reality of many who dare not admit that we are being forced to love a God who is always angry at us, who cannot be pleased, who heaps shame upon us, and often our only relief from this unbearable reality is the very "sin" that drives our shame. If not that, it is imperative to work ourselves to death. *Hearts to*

A Christian Ethic for the Modern Church

God, hands to work. McCarraher laments, "Obliged by nature to acquire omnipotence over nature and their own desires, the American descendants of the Puritan idealized a ferocious and aesthetically analgesic productivity. Insensitive to beauty, reproachful of idleness, and obsessed with sin and decline, Puritans imparted to subsequent generations an abhorrence of sheer delight."[1]

Genesis tells us that what God made was and is very good. Romans chapter 1 teaches us that God's creation is the general revelation of himself to humanity, that we may understand through its grandeur, beauty, and complexity that there is some "person" behind it all. We are without excuse. See also Psalm 19. But many have denied and refused this revelation and closed our hearts to the truth. So often, in our quest for "orthodoxy," we in the Church have disregarded this general revelation of God in his creation as some sort of idolatrous animism, little realizing that for the Christian especially, the created order should be held in the highest esteem. It is *our* God's property. It bears his imprint. It is his gift to us, and in contrast to accusations of animism, I submit that our attitudes and behavior toward the created order are indicative of our internal psychology and spiritual state.

The created order includes our bodies, and their expression in our families and marriages, our sexuality, and our interior giftings. Dorothy Sayers suggests that it includes our creative capacity, calling it the very essence of the *imago Dei*.

Another extreme of the deification of the material is that we are enchanted by the matter itself, and not just in what we would consider animism, paganism, or the carving of an idol to bow down to. We accumulate money and possessions heedless of Jesus' parable of the bigger barns, and heedless of the fact that as we as a society take everything, there are people on the other end getting less or nothing. There are people on the other end making these things, often in inhumane conditions, and often for little or no pay. The material products our society buys in great quantity, and often out of a compulsion to quiet our spiritual pain, are made by other human beings. We must consider if we can hold to the integrity of our Christian confession as these dynamics come to light. We must consider the spiritual poverty that necessitates a need to constantly consume.

Human beings are "unities" of body and spirit, material and immaterial. We have discussed some of the perceptive distortions as concern the material, and we will return to those themes as we go. The problem I wish to address overall in this chapter, however, is our tendency to minimize or deny this spiritual aspect of our reality. The Enlightenment and the Industrial and Technological revolutions have delivered to humanity a devastating skepticism regarding things spiritual. This was aided by our major wars, the vacuity of the Christian spiritual life as observed by the "hippie" generation who rebelled against it, and the false dichotomy of science or "reason" with spiritual belief. These are just a few examples of many. The modern Church must be able to demonstrate a reliance on the objective reality of God and his faithfulness while being able to articulate his truth which is indeed reasonable. The more we come into alignment with this truth, the closer we are to being empowered by and flowing from our true Source, and the more we are able to discern and practice meaningful life and action. The Church is without a doubt able to provide the world with answers about the here and the hereafter, and a clearly articulated worldview that does no violence to true reason. This is a great need in our generation, but the soil of the Church must first be recovered from the spirit of this age. We will consider the nature of our membership in the Kingdom of God.

When we responded in the affirmative to the conviction of the Holy Spirit, and the truth of the Gospel, we joined the kingdom of God, body, mind, and spirit. (I will not discuss the doctrines of salvation, baptism, and sanctification here, vital as they are, so that I may not divert from the current point.) Ephesians 2:19 states, "So then you are no longer strangers and aliens, but you are fellow citizens with the saints and members of the household of God . . ." Further, 1 Peter states, "But ye are a chosen generation, a royal priesthood, a holy nation, a peculiar people . . ." (1 Peter 2:9, KJV).

The existence of this "Kingdom of God" presents us with some formidable difficulties. Let us look at John 18:36, "Jesus answered, 'My kingdom is not of this world. If my kingdom were of this world, my servants would have been fighting, that I might not be delivered over to the Jews. But my kingdom is not from the world.'" Jesus will later inform Pilate that he (Pilate) would have no authority at all if it had not been granted by God. In this apparent paradox, Jesus is standing before the secular government and the religious leadership of his day. It is exactly at this point in life that so many of us choose to fight with our fists, not understanding that above and beyond all of our unavoidable physicality and mediated through it, but *not exclusively governed by it*, is the spiritual reality unseen, the wicked but limited forces that oppose the will of God and animate and influence the kingdoms of this world. But further still is the sovereign plan and purpose of God, hidden from the audience at the time, but evident to those of us who have the privilege of reading the account in Scripture after the fact.

The drama as viewed by the crowds and rulers in the gospel

account of Jesus' trial was that of a "malefactor and rabble-rouser," as it has been said, spreading strange doctrines and claiming to be the Son of God. Here, the religious leaders have unwittingly delivered their Messiah to the secular government to be disposed of. All of hell is rejoicing. Again, we have the benefit of hindsight. The Scripture states, "Which none of the princes of this world knew: for had they known it, they would not have crucified the Lord of glory" (1 Cor 2:8, KJV). See the entire letter! Are the events of our lives, of our world and time, any different? Isaiah 55 tells us that God's ways and thoughts are higher than ours. He tells us to, "Trust in the Lord with all your heart, and do not lean on your own understanding. In all your ways acknowledge him, and he will make straight your paths" (Proverbs 3:5-6). Romans 12:2 tells us, "Do not be conformed to this world, but be transformed by the renewal of your mind, that by testing you may discern what is the will of God, what is good and acceptable and perfect." The first epistle of John says, "For all that is in the world, the lust of the flesh, the lust of the eyes, and the pride of life, is not of the Father, but is of the world" (1 John 2:16, KJV). We must grow to trust in the sovereignty, the faithfulness, and the mystery of God while taking faithful action in this life.

This is the proper meeting of spirit and body, through the renewing of the mind, through prayer, through trusting in the objectively real person of God, and his willingness and ability to mediate and direct the events of our lives. When we realize that we are members of God's kingdom, we can begin to position ourselves properly for the kingdoms, powers, and principalities of this world. It is grievous to see professing Christians with acrid political signs and bumper stickers in a society as viciously divided by politics as ours. As salt and light, we must ask ourselves if we are indeed engaging in meaningful political processes in the love of Christ, or if we are expressing bitterness, fear, and misplaced trust more than anything else. Have we considered the grievances of our enemies? Have we met with them face to face in the spirit of Christ? It is a tall order indeed!

Regarding many of these issues, I suspect that we are not unique as a culture. However, the kingdom of God is supposed to be an *evident* antidote and alternative to the kingdoms and systems of this world, yet we keep seeking hope in earthly institutions. Doing so leads many to seek power in ungodly ways. We have done likewise throughout history with the Enlightenment and the Industrial and Technological revolutions. We have deified this entity we call "SCIENCE." These misplaced hopes and their attendant behaviors can create damage to the witness of the Church. There is certainly good that can come from each of the institutions named above, and Christianity should not equal anti-intellectualism, but we must operate first and foremost under the objective reality of the God we profess. The strident tone of these objections stems not from a desire to demonize knowledge, production, or scientific inquiry, but from observing the severity of the human temptation to indulge in them to devastating effect.

What should the Christian position be regarding politics? Craig Slane observes, "Christian martyrdom always has political overtones because it is where the kingdom of God and the kingdoms of this world collide."[2] So, it is obvious that there will be an unavoidable interface. It is the nature of this interface that we need to look at. DeGruchy continues, "Jesus' eventual silence in response to Pilate's questioning is the loudest possible expression of 'speaking truth to power' because it is a refusal to acknowledge such power as supreme."³ Contrast this with some of the political activism being perpetrated currently under the auspices of Christianity, whereby we seek an alliance with and control of our government institutions instead of being a witness to, with, and often against them.

Consider the civil rights movement of the 1960s. Through much prayer and planning, through many mistakes, and through much trial, Dr. Martin Luther King Jr and many other like-minded leaders enacted a powerful, non-violent revolution that changed the course of the nation forever. Reverend King spoke to some of the psychology thus, "Instead of submitting to surreptitious cruelty in thousands of dark jail cells and on countless shadowed street corners, he would force his oppressor to commit his brutality openly in the light of day with the rest of the world looking on."⁴ Instead of attempting to infiltrate and influence the state from the inside, and instead of spewing hateful political rhetoric, they shined the light of truth on injustice. They suffered in the process, but ultimately, they gained much, and left an example for the Church to follow. NT Wright says, ". . . we can speak perfectly credibly in our own day too of the power of the kingdom of the risen Jesus to overthrow proud and oppressive regimes, and to give hope to the humble and poor, and to do so with remarkable restraint, dignity, justice, and peace."⁵

With all the gains made during the civil rights movement, it is plain that our world is a broken place still riddled with oppression, injustice, and exploitation. This is where the Christian must trust in God while pursuing the good and the right in his or her actions. It is God who "works all things after the counsel of his own will" (Eph 1:11). Likewise, we must gain a greater understanding of the overall purposes of God for us and his world. We *can* expect to make a significant impact, as our history shows. We can also expect setbacks, failures, and unmet expectations. This world will not be perfect until Jesus returns.

God's kingdom is sovereign over all. It is this kingdom into which we have been adopted. It operates differently than the kingdoms of this world, and we are called to come out of the world and be separate. See Rev 18:4, 2 Cor 6:17, and Jer 51. This is not an admonition to physical isolation; it is a call to an empowered life in God. This work is hopefully an exposition and an expansion of this concept. Let us proceed first to the primary vehicle through which the kingdom of God is brought to bear on our human condition.

2

PRAYER

"When I shut up the heavens so that there is no rain, or command the locust to devour the land, or send pestilence among my people, if my people who are called by my name humble themselves, and pray and seek my face and turn from their wicked ways, then I will hear from heaven and will forgive their sin and heal their land" (2 Chronicles 7:13-14).

cf: Is 58, Rev 5:8, Lu18:1-8, Ja 5:13-18, 1 Thess 5:17, Eph 6:18, Phil 4:6, Acts 1:14, Dan 9:3-19

Prayer is meant to be *the* fundamental Christian action, although the word "action" does not adequately express the reality of prayer. We see from the scripture above that prayer is an action, a posture of humility, and a life of constant repentance. It is unceasing communion with God. We see in Ephesians 6:12-18 that prayer is the objective reality of our spiritual warfare. In other words, prayer makes things happen "in the spirit," which then makes things happen in what we call the natural, to use the regrettable false dichotomy. Prayer is a primary mechanism through which we experience repentance, change, comfort, and the spiritual sustenance by which we live.

It changes us. Prayer covers all. In the above passage, and in Isaiah 58, we see answered prayer within the context of not only repentance but of social justice and acts of mercy. There is a holistic principle at work here, and in this section, I wish to look at the function of prayer within the whole of life.

Untold volumes have been written about prayer by people far more spiritual than myself. I would refer you to their works to learn the mechanics of prayer, the most important of which is to do it without ceasing! I would encourage all of us to learn prayer individually and in community. In this section, however, I would like to look at returning prayer to its proper place within the whole of our experience. Like the difficulties we discussed in the last section over spirit and matter, prayer is one of those things that tends to get sidelined by what we often consider in our hearts to be the "real" action of life. We are too busy to pray. There are "more important" things that need to be done. But, building on a return to the objective reality of our God, and the trustworthiness of his Word, it is possible to construct an ethic of prayer *as action*, and prayer in concert with action. Within this ethic are a return to balance, peace, meaning, and effectiveness.

Prayer should be the default mode of life for the Christian. It is the putting on of the yoke of Christ. In the process of prayer, we transfer the burdens, the needs, and the anxieties of this life onto God who alone can bear them. 1 Thessalonians 5:17 counsels us to pray without ceasing. Philippians 4:6-7 states, "... do not be anxious about anything, but in everything with prayer and supplication with thanksgiving let your requests be made known to God. And the peace of God, which surpasses all understanding, will guard your hearts and minds in Christ Jesus." Similar to God's command to a Sabbath and all that entails, submission to a life of prayer is rest. It is being the truest to our nature as his children. There is in this life of prayer the potential for substantial relief from anxiety, depression, and many manifestations of mental illness and exhaustion. This is illustrated in the well-known story of Mary and Martha in Luke chapter 10. We find Mary at the feet of Jesus, hearing his words, and we find Martha, "... anxious and troubled about many things." This sounds precisely like so many of us. One thing is needful, Jesus says.

The book of Daniel is an extended illustration of the sovereignty of God over world affairs and its main human character, Daniel, is seen praying throughout, while for us the veil is pulled back a bit so we can see what is spiritually taking place. See Daniel 9:3-19. Daniel's prayers were heard, and God was answering long before the answers became apparent, and we see that this delay was because of the spiritual forces engaged in the affairs of heaven and earth. Daniel's prayers were instrumental in bringing about earthly events.

Before activism, speaking truth to power, or making changes, should be prayer. It should be considered the action before the action. It is, again, the foundational action. Prayer is the attitude of humility before God, *your* kingdom come, *your* will be done. Jesus often resorted to a solitary place to pray to his Father. How much more should we, who still bear the sting and vestige of our sinful nature until he returns for us?

James 5:13-18 tells us that prayer works. It causes things to happen. It is medicine to our affliction, our sickness, our sins, and again (vs. 17-18), the primary vehicle through which we act in this world. We can trust that God is sovereign over national affairs and the affairs of our individual lives. This is why we can and should relax our grip on the political apparatus. It is not nearly as important who is "in office" as who is in office in our hearts. It is why we can be released from the need to control everyone and everything around us, which is the essence of fear and codependency. It is exhausting!

The entire Hebrew testament is the story of God's continual calling of his people to holiness, his judgment of wickedness, and the outworking of his eschatological plan to provide his Son to humanity. Jesus came as an example of holiness and life, and as the sacrifice to reconcile us to himself through his death and resurrection. See 2 Cor 5. God has got us covered, past, present, and future. Understanding this allows us to find rest in his sovereignty. In this mindset, our life of prayer changes from one of duty, desperation, or drudgery to one of abiding communion and relationship. This, in turn, affects our health and our outlook. It affects how we interact with the world, even in its broken state.

The incarnation of Jesus gives us further insight into the nature of prayer. Hebrews 2:17 states, "Therefore he had to be made like his brothers in every respect, so that he might become a merciful and faithful high priest in the service of God, to make propitiation for the sins of the people." In this, we begin to see God's intention. It is the joining of divinity into humanity, and into the experience of humanity, that Jesus undertook, that gives us a profound illustration of the intention and spirit of prayer. Simply put, we *spend ourselves* in communion with God. We join with him in his work, and his love. We exercise the relationship he has offered us. It requires the very real commodities of time, effort, intensity, and emotion. Let us keep in mind these ideas of joining, and of relationship throughout this work, as they are the seeds of the entire theme.

Without prayer and a proper understanding of the kingdom of God, our only options are to exercise self-effort and self-will to make our way in the world. Many people feel a great sense of confidence in their ability to conquer life on their own, but even the most "successful" human beings on the planet will meet with us in death. They will meet with us in suffering and tragedy. The author of Ecclesiastes lamented that "time and chance happen to them all" (Ecc 9:11). With the spiritual poverty of prayerlessness, and the lack of a vital connection to God, we must force our will upon the world. That holds true in our intimate human relationships, our workplaces, and our attempts at wrangling life out of the political and economic apparatus. We become manipulative. We become despondent. We become fearful, angry, and insular. This leads us away from the Agape love of Jesus

We must also acknowledge the power of the human impulse to worship. It is how we are made. Human beings have innate compulsions to devotion, affection, and relationships, and the reality is that *all things* that are not God will cause harm when they are worshiped out of order. This misplacement of affection is the cause of untold mental, spiritual, and physical illness. It is a major cause of relational dysfunction. The remedy for so much of our sickness, our addictions and compulsions, and perhaps even our need for so many medications, is time with and a living relationship with our loving God. Other factors come to bear here as well, such as a properly functioning, intimate, organic Christian community. We will develop this element further on in the work.

Isaiah chapter 58 bears study and meditation. It is obvious

from numerous verses in this passage that there is indeed an earnest religious function taking place. See verse 2. The people are wondering why their prayers are going unheeded, their fasts are not being respected. God has several indictments against the people: they are oppressing their workers (v3,6), they are engaging in violence, and, by implication, an angry or hateful spirit (vs 4,6,9). They are neglecting acts of love and mercy (vs 6-7, 10). They are neglecting the Sabbath commandment of the Lord (v13).

While this may seem to contradict the main point of prayer being the action before the action, I must reiterate that, as a human being is a unity of body and spirit, so the action of prayer is an inseparable element of the unified life of holiness, love, justice, and mercy which is God's design for his people. This chapter in Isaiah illustrates the spirit of prayer, communion with God wedded to compassionate action and the development of an inner spirit of peace. God's call to observe his Sabbath is the proper posture of trust, rest, and the enjoyment of his provision. It is the end of the fearful ethos of scarcity.

Further study of the chapter reveals God's desire for us when our prayer and action are rightly ordered. He promises us light, healing, and answered prayers. He offers us guidance, inner fulfillment, and strength, even in the dry times. Verse 12 is an incredible promise of restoration. If God's people will sanctify themselves to prayer and a right spirit, to a compassionate life, God will empower us to repair his house and witness the Body of Christ to our generation. This is a fundamental need of our time. It begins with each of us.

In light of these thoughts, we must evaluate our brand of action in this world, and where prayer may bring healing. Randall Balmer observes, "Evangelicals need once again to learn to be a counterculture ... before they succumbed to the seductions of power [Jesus' followers] were a counterculture because they stood apart from the prevailing order. A counterculture can provide a critique of the powerful because it is utterly disinterested-it has no investment in the power structure itself."[1] As an example he goes on to issue a challenge to the Church to juxtapose the Sermon on the Mount with the discourse of the "religious right."

Through a distinct series of historical events, much of the Church in America has chosen the path of political influence from within, rather than Kingdom of God influence from without. This has led to compromise, and fear-based ideologies that have nothing to do with the spirit of Christ and the gospel. We will expound on this theme further as we go, speaking more specifically, but let us lay out the rudiments of a principle. In the absence of a robust life of prayer within the body of Christ, we have no choice but to play politics. We set up bogey-men outside the walls of the church. We seek to impute morality only through law and politics, rather than love and truth. The very real power and Agape made available to us in Christ, exercised in prayer and loving action, should be our primary tool for change, and not an afterthought.

At the same time, we have excused and overlooked many endemic moral issues *within* the Church. Have we as a Body exerted the same intensity of activism within to set our own house in order?

Although many of the works and causes of the body of Christ are good, right, and commended to us by God himself, (See Eph 2:10), they are not the full expression of the gospel and are not to replace the spiritual work of prayer. If anything, we see in our scriptural examples that good works are meant to work in concert with fervent prayer and righteous living.

A Christian Ethic for the Modern Church

We must further understand that Christian ministry and activism are directed toward entirely different ends than those of the world. 2 Corinthians 2:15-16, KJV, states, "For we are unto God a sweet savour of Christ, in them that are saved, and in them that perish: To the one we are the savour of death unto death; and to the other the savour of life unto life. And who is sufficient for these things?" Who indeed! It is incumbent upon the Church to bear witness to the truth, that all the world is guilty before God, that there is a just judgment coming, and that there is a remedy for our human predicament. See Romans 1:20, 3:19. John 18:37 states, "Pilate said, 'So you are a king?' Jesus responded, 'You say that I am a king. For this purpose I was born and for this purpose I have come into the world, to bear witness to the truth.'" We are "little Christs" bearing this same witness by speaking the truth and by *non-transactional* acts of love, performed from a deep foundation of intimacy with God. This cannot happen without prayer. Human beings cannot bear up to the demands of the gospel without prayer. This is what separates the gospel of Christ from humanistic activism, the spiritual element. Unfortunately, we have often throughout history become utilitarian in our evangelism, seeking to manufacture converts rather than drawing those human *unities* into a life within the Body. NT Wright rightly observes that the great divide of Christianity is evangelism to save souls for a timeless eternity, rather than a mission of working for justice, peace, and hope in the present world. He calls it enslavement to the Platonic ideology of the Enlightenment, which we discussed in the last chapter.[2] He goes on to say that we are ". . . saved as wholes, not souls."[3] Therefore, we may begin to heal our thinking by looking at both as one ministry of the body of Christ on this earth, and not as irreconcilable ideologies.

Prayer

We need not over-spiritualize the virtues of simple kindness, generosity, and living innocently and simply in this world. As Christians, we are free to "practice" the fruit of the Spirit without end. See Galatians 5. See the epistle of James also, for practical instruction on speech, giving, wealth, and the inner spirit that should animate the people of God. See the book of Acts. In fact, it is just this "primitive communism" that seems to be most effective in drawing people to Christ, the meeting of basic needs, the attention paid to the marginalized, the absorption of people into an organic community, the sharing of Biblical truth in a context of genuine concern.

Last, we understand the fullest purposes of God's admonition to the great commandments. Our sanctification, the process in this life by which we become conformed to his image, is part and parcel of our lives, prayer, and action. We are part of God's overarching and eternal plan for his creation. His plan includes the purification of his Bride, the Church, the dissolution of this present order, and the establishment of his eternal fellowship with us in glorified bodies, in a new heaven and a new earth. It is this eschatological hope which should animate us and motivate us to set our compass to true north. It should inform us. This is why we can work for the good with all intensity, still avoiding the prevalent notion that this world is perfectible by us in this age. God's plans and purposes are *not* those of this current world order; neither should ours be. We have to want what God wants. We must be willing to trust, and it requires trust not to need to dominate the structures of power in this present world. To want what God wants requires prayer and the renewal of our minds.

In our next chapter, we will engage with the human realities we face as individuals in our modern society. We will engage with our psychology, our ethos, and our history that we may evaluate who we've been, who we are, and who we might become as Christians in this current generation. It is hoped that by undergoing the sometimes-painful surgeries of introspection, examination, and illumination, we may then be able to develop a salutary ethic. This will not only heal many of our spiritual maladies, but will begin to repair our witness to the wider world and increase our experience of meaningful engagement.

3
ON THE CHRISTIAN IN THE WORLD

Having acknowledged the existence of our spiritual reality and the need for prayer as *the* foundational act of the Christian, we define the primary impulse of the Christian ethic as a call to holiness. Philippians 2:15-16 states, "... that you may be blameless and innocent, children of God without blemish in the midst of a crooked and twisted generation, among whom you shine as lights in the world, holding fast to the word of life ..." Implicit in the phrase "blameless and innocent," is the call to holiness expressed in part by what we might call simplicity. We will expound on this theme as we proceed. It is certainly fundamental *for such a time as this.*

Innocence is not ignorance. In fact, we need the very opposite of ignorance, so that we may have a clear understanding of our current crises. Is it possible that complicity in the sins of our fathers, so to speak, compromise with materialism, consumerism, and affluence, and the manner of our engagement with this current generation has

A Christian Ethic for the Modern Church

cost us any moral high ground, or any *pulpit* from which to speak to the wider world? Is the Western church equipped to engage those on the margins with the truth of Christ? Do we have mechanisms in place to develop Christian community among people for whom the church is utterly foreign? Is it possible that many people are waking up to and balking at the "church as corporation" model? I have met many people who will not abide it anymore, and there are perhaps more who should not.

Before, we sought to reorient our understanding of the whole of our physical and spiritual reality, and the need for a radical change in how we "take action." Now, we must deconstruct certain generations-deep and prevalent mindsets within the body of Christ. It is a difficult task riddled with terrifying implications, but one that the Christian must undertake. The task is this: to face squarely the history and the current mechanics of our Church, nation, and selves. It is to make those necessary adjustments at the corporate and personal levels to bring our lives and actions most into harmony with the spirit of Christ and the ethos of the Scriptures, rightly divided. It is to repair the Church *within me* and *us* so that we are a viable destination, a home, for the human being who comes to us to flourish. It is to make progress toward blamelessness and innocence, that none would reject Christ on account of distortions in this thing we call the church, and not on account of the individual Christian who has been so absorbed into the spirit of this age that he or she has no living witness, no joy, and nothing to offer the wider world. It is to plead with every Christian to lay up more treasure in heaven, and less on earth.

On the element of the Scripture, one might argue that it has been used to justify all manner of evil, to promote the very opposite of human flourishing through manifold channels and one would be correct. One would also rightly argue that the Protestant church has thousands of sects and divisions, that the Roman church has at times been plagued by scandals and compromise, and that "conservative" religious extremism has, as the Scripture states, given occasion to those outside the Church to blaspheme. See Romans 2:24. How could any consistent ethic be derived amid these realities? Add to that the advent of globalism, the changing moral and philosophical landscape of our nation, and the growing dissatisfaction with our power structures, and we see that the task before us is difficult indeed. The concerns are relevant. I would first submit, however, that the primary difficulties we face inside the Church spring from the endemic and persistent violation of the clearest mandates of Scripture, about which there should be little argument. There is no need to seek out esoteric interpretations, obscure doctrines, or bogey-men outside in the wider world. What if, for example, we were to juxtapose the ten commandments, the sermon on the mount, and the two greatest commandments with our personal lives and the manner of our church organization? What about Galatians 5, Colossians 3, and the entire epistle of James?

We have so often failed the great commandments to love God and our neighbor. Romans 13:10, KJV states, "Love worketh no ill to his neighbor: therefore love is the fulfilling of the law." This failure has manifested itself through several primary avenues, which we will examine in turn before we suggest the development of a salutary ethic for the individual Christian. Although much of this material could be applied corporately as well, we will focus more fully on the Church as an institution in the next chapter.

First of all, the fallout and devastation wrought by the spirit of *mammon*, (we could as well use the term *covetousness*) cannot be calculated. It is a primary spiritual disease of humanity. It has brought forth almost every social evil and intractable problem we now face. It is that very Babylon described in the Revelation, "With whom the kings of the earth have committed fornication, and the inhabitants of the earth have been made drunk with the wine of her fornication" (Rev 17:2 KJV). The apostle John continues, "And I saw the woman, drunk with the blood of the saints, the blood of the martyrs of Jesus" (Rev 17:6). How tragic for God's people to drink from the same cup! See also verse 18:24.

Chapters 17 and 18 of the Revelation describe in detail the judgment of "Babylon." It is easy to dismiss this book of the Bible due to its symbolic and often mysterious nature, so in our case, I would like to start with what is obvious and observable from these chapters. Let us look at *what* is being described, compare it to our own realities, and then draw conclusions and principles consistent with the rest of Scripture, reason, and with history.

Revelation 18:3, KJV states, "For all nations have drunk of the wine of the wrath of her fornication, and the kings of the earth have committed fornication with her, and the merchants of the earth are waxed rich through the abundance of her delicacies." Let us affirm that in this we are not dealing solely with an "American" problem. It is a human problem with spiritual underpinnings. The problem as concerns us is that this spirit has infiltrated the Western Church in no small measure. I contend, along with others, that this spirit of mammon, or covetousness, was foundational to the establishment of our society. I contend further that the Church's intentional, and so often unintentional complicity with it has continued to this day, causing grievous harm to our witness and the spiritual health of Christians. Revelation 18:4-5 continues, "Then I heard another voice from heaven saying, 'Come out of her, my people, lest you take part in her sins, lest you share in her plagues; for her sins are heaped high as heaven, and God has remembered her iniquities.'" This admonition is directed specifically toward the people of God, in the context of his intended judgment toward the evil world system of covetousness and immoral expressions of commerce.

These two chapters are explicit in their indictment of commerce, political and economic corruption, and human exploitation. Let us not read commerce as evil in principle, but as evil in practice when devoid of the presence of God and his moral framework. Any honest accounting will reveal how overwhelming and ubiquitous is this evil expression. The Scripture shows us that environmental exploitation is connected and will bring judgment as well. See Revelation 11:18, Romans 8, Isaiah 24:4-6, Ezekiel 34:2-4, and Jeremiah 2:7. We will develop these themes in connection with the proliferation of the gospel as we progress.

Practically speaking, how has this been manifested in our society, and what is to be done? We must do the hard work of facing the ugly parts of our past and present, and the ingrained psychology within which we operate as a modern, affluent culture, often unaware of what is going on in the world, and how we are being *taught* a particular narrative by our schools, governments, "news" outlets, and entertainment media. It would seem helpful to encourage understanding within the body of Christ and develop a willingness on the part of each of us to consider truth and reality in all their ramifications. It is one thing to know our history. It is quite another to enter into the reality of it, the persistent consequences of it, and the humanity of those who are directly affected by it. It becomes even more difficult, yet necessary, to face the confluence of *me* with injustice, complicity, and damage to the witness of Christ. It should be understood that none of us is directly responsible for the actions of our forebears, lest we take on distorted and nebulous guilt that allows our critics to keep us imprisoned in a lose-lose situation. Many in our modern milieu would demonize Christians and white people as perpetual colonialists and racists, among other things. This is a belligerent mindset that leads only to further division. Contrariwise, for modern Christians to turn a blind eye to our inherited psychology, to refuse to take responsibility for our actions in this world, is in a measure to affirm the accusations. This is true for the Western Church and her children, and just as true for every affluent nation on earth.

I contend that the process of discovery can but end in certain despair. None of us wishes to wallow in human misery and atrocity, nor is it a healthy habit. The problem is that so many of us have insulated ourselves from reality altogether, or we have displaced it. As long as it is happening *over there* or *back then* it is not something I have to think about. Another form of our denial is the narrative, the myth, that all is well here, and that we are innocent of the kind of evildoing which we sometimes accuse other nations of with impunity. It is incumbent, and biblical, for all of us to seek an understanding of reality, until we are seeing this world as it is. See 2 Thes 2:10-11, Rom 1:18, 25, Jer 7:28, 1 Jn 1:8. Without a doubt, the Christian needs to pass through this valley of despair, again, not that we should wallow in it, but that we should turn our trust from the powers and institutions of this world to God and his eschatological reality. It might do every Christian good to be afflicted with a sense of deep and abiding sadness at

On the Christian in the World

the world's reality versus the active practice of a life of denial. "It is better to go to the house of mourning than to go to the house of feasting..." (Ecc 7:2). Facing reality also enables us to see the profound need all around us, in the low places as well as the affluent society, and take action. See James 4:9, Ecclesiastes 7:2, Isaiah 58, and 2 Cor 7:10. And, in the taking of action we may find a new experience of transcendence, ministry, and meaning, something many of us could use.

Because we are God's people, we can bring holistic hope to the despairing. That is something simple humanism cannot fully do, although this point will be argued. In some aspects the argument is legitimate, although to build that case would be a lengthy endeavor. As passionate and good-hearted as so many activists are, as powerful, important, and righteous as their works are, they often lack the truth of the human condition and the eternal answer that is to be found only in the revelation of Jesus. Indeed, I submit that much of the passion of their activism is in the cause itself because this world and earth are all they have. When the cause, the earth, and their life is gone, it is all over. In sad contrast to so many of us, these citizens and activists often have a much more profound understanding of the value of creation and human life. Has the modern church jettisoned these exalted virtues in exchange for *stuff*? We may lay claim to the sanctity of life as a Church-held virtue by some of our often-misguided political activism, but our history and the realities of our consumerism militate against this. Fortunately, many people are waking up to these truths. See 1 Thes 4:13.

As I contemplate my status as a Christian in this world, I must consider the words of Jesus who said, "But you will receive power when the Holy Spirit has come upon you, and you will be my witnesses in Jerusalem and in all Judea and

A Christian Ethic for the Modern Church

Samaria, and to the end of the earth" (Acts 1:8). It is manifest in the scripture that we Christians are here for a reason. Ephesians 2:10 states, "For we are his workmanship, created in Christ Jesus for good works, which God prepared beforehand, that we should walk in them." Is there congruency between my presence in this world, the power of the Holy Spirit, and the foreordained works of God? In confronting history and truth, it is important to keep in mind our purpose, which is the integration of our identity as the people of God with our reality in practice.

The first part of our "waking up," and the deconstruction of harmful myths was addressed in the last chapter. It is a return to the understanding of our "revolutionary" status in the world, to the fact that we belong ultimately to God and not the State, and we are and can be empowered through prayer and loving action to be a force for good in this age, knowing that God has the final say, not the world, the devil, or the State. We need not be discouraged by this world which ". . . lies in wickedness" (1 John 5:19). Neither do we have an excuse to be deluded or complacent. Each Christian has a special mission to fulfill with his or her time here. We must be about the Father's business and do those works God has ordained for us from eternity past. See Luke 2:49 and Eph 2:10. Let us take note that "being about the Father's business," so to speak, is how we fulfill the deep yearnings of our hearts, lest we hear only drudgery in these admonitions and considerations. Jesus said, "Whoever finds his life will lose it, and whoever loses his life for my sake will find it" (Matt 10:39).

As "modern" as I may consider myself, I have contemplated that I am only one generation removed from segregated schools

On the Christian in the World

and buses, from the persistent institutional demoralization that has affected African-American people for hundreds of years.

Our society is so constructed that I participate in oppression, injustice, and even self-injury almost every time I open my wallet to buy something, choose something to eat, or choose what to feed my mind.

Before the arrival of the Europeans, North America was already home to around four hundred distinct societies of people, totaling around 7 to 10 million persons.[1] For untold generations they managed the land and forests harmoniously. We will paint them as human, to be sure, but let us realize the lingering impact of labeling them "savages." It is inaccurate and disingenuous to say that this land was "discovered" in any sense. Statements I have even heard even within the last year to the effect that we "tamed this continent" are indicative of a certain psychological denial, or refusal to face facts. This continent was taken from the indigenous people by violence, and the nature of that violence is no less hideous than any atrocity the world over. Dispossession of native people from their lands, forced relocations, the decimation of food supplies through slaughter, forced "Christianization" and "Europeanization." Native people were placed in camps. Their family and tribal units were torn apart. They were forced to abandon their languages and customs. They were subject to a farcical treaty system. They were subject to diseases that decimated their populations. Many were tortured. They were subjected to a means of warfare intended to eradicate them, a concept utterly foreign to Native Americans whose belief structure encompassed the sanctity of the entire cosmos, humans, animals, resources, the created order, and even their enemies. It is interesting to note that the early settlers had significant problems with Europeans leaving to go live with the Natives, but not the other way around. Why? I think answering this question will yield incredible and necessary insights to us as a modern society.

Derrick Jensen laments, "To this day the federal government admits that thirty-three percent of the land mass of the continental United States was never ceded by treaty and, therefore, is held illegally."[2] What about the other sixty-seven percent? Jensen goes on regarding so many of the Europeans, "They came also to enslave the land, to yoke it to their own purpose, and ultimately to remove from it everything of monetary value."[3] I would argue that we only have state and federal lands because a small minority of people in the right places wanted to preserve *something* so the continent would not be completely denuded. And now, of course, nearly every other acre is "private property" and thus inaccessible to most of us. Contrast this with the "right to roam" ethos of Norway, for example. I must ask what people mean when they use the word "freedom." A fitting survey of this period of our history would fill many volumes. Christian people would do well to seek out the truth.

Likewise, much of the "reeducation" of the Native Americans was done under the supposed auspices of the Church. We as a Church must understand this, even when Christianity and the Scripture were used in a disingenuous manner. Native Americans still suffer the fallout of these injustices. We must not only understand the particulars of our history, but we must understand the psychology that would lead the Church of God into this sort of action. It is relevant today, at the very least, that vestiges of these things manifest themselves in racism, mistrust, and paternalistic ministry and mission work.

On the Christian in the World

We must confront the psychology of *Manifest Destiny* and the idea of the United States being a new Israel, thus justifying the above-mentioned atrocities. We ask ourselves at what point does long occupation and use equal ownership and authority, and prepare for the terror of a question that seems to yield no comforting answers. What is our responsibility toward the indigenous inhabitants of this land? Why should such questions matter to the modern Christian? What does it matter to me what happened so many hundreds of years ago? Is it possible that the psychologies passed down from our forebears are part and parcel of how we see the world? Of how we "do" what we call ministry? How much of our current policy is continuing to cause harm to Native peoples and others because it is not a factor in our deliberations? Is it possible that understanding and locating ourselves as a people historically, and a change in these ways of seeing could open vast new opportunities for healing and reconciliation, for a new fundamental psychology of ministry, one closer to the heart of Jesus?

We must face the horrors of slavery in all their gruesomeness, and the use of the Bible and the gospel to further subjugate the African slaves. One would rightly argue that as the apostle Paul says, "They are not all Israel, who are called Israel" (Romans 9:6). I must conclude that very few, if any, of those who participated in the atrocities against the native Americans, or the African slaves, even under the auspices of the Bible or Church, were actually *Christian*. It is unconscionable to me that a Christian, a human being in whom the Spirit of God dwells could practice chattel slavery or genocide. But again, even where we are not at fault, the effects linger.

It cannot be doubted, however, that even amidst the

A Christian Ethic for the Modern Church

turmoil of colonization and the Industrial Revolution, there were Christian people who were here of a good and right heart. This has, I believe, been true of the Church since its inception. Let the wheat and the tares grow together until the end. See Acts 1:8. See Matthew 13:30.

This still leaves us with some disturbing realities. What about the silent Christians? Those who refused to make a stand against such atrocities? Several prominent religious leaders have been reported as tragically absent during the civil rights movement of the 1960s. How might our present be different if the full weight of the American church had been behind Dr. King and his companions? He lamented most fully about those he termed "white moderates" who always sought to be a part of the good once "a more convenient season" arrived.[4] He mentioned, "... the appalling silence of good people."[5] We have observed what happened in Germany before and during World War 2, how the church was subsumed by the Nazi party, oftentimes eagerly, and how the likes of Karl Barth and Dietrich Bonhoeffer had to make a stand, calling forth a "Confessing Church" to reaffirm the truth of Christ and stand for it. What about us, today? Again, we make our position known by how we choose to live, how we choose to spend our time and money, and how we steward what God has created and given to us.

The Church is the edifice to the presence of God in our communities, yet we face complicity with racism and a continuing sort of self-imposed segregation. These issues are complex beyond measure, but what is to prevent me from walking across the tracks? Likewise, the buzzwords (and they are not just buzzwords now, they are full-blown societal movements, en route to a dangerous regime of modern totalitarianism, and the end of the civil rights they claim to champion) of diversity and globalism seem good to many, threatening to others. However, it would seem that these "goals" are more political than anything and misguided on other levels. What we call Diversity often boils down to an anti-European, anti-white program designed to eliminate free speech, stop open debate, and end what we might call the Judeo-Christian ethic. This is evidenced in the increasing proliferation of mandatory workplace trainings, required agreements, the nature of our entertainment media, dangerous ideologies being propagated in the universities, the subsuming of corporate America by cultural movements, the punishment of dissenters, and the constant outrage proliferated by "news" and social media networks.

Should not the Church pursue a robust heterogeneity in a different spirit? A recognition of the value and humanity of each other, no matter who we are? We must indeed venture outside the walls of our churches with haste. We must get to know the brothers and sisters "on the other side of the tracks." But this must work in every direction, and be done with the love of God.

We would do well to promote the fellowship of the Spirit. James 3:18 KJV states, "And the fruit of righteousness is sown in peace of them that make peace." The doors of our churches should be open to anyone without discrimination. The Church moving forward will be required to be conversant among many different communities of people. I submit that this can be done without fear or compromise of one's internal convictions. It can be done without capitulating the Church and the Kingdom of God to the loudest demands of the culture. God is faithful. It requires hard work to build relationships with people who are different from us and to be patient with their afflictions and imperfections. Of course, they must bear with us as well!

2 Timothy 2:24-26 states: "And the Lord's servant must not be quarrelsome but kind to everyone, able to teach, patiently enduring evil, correcting his opponents with gentleness. God may perhaps grant them repentance leading to a knowledge of the truth and they may come to their senses and escape from the snare of the devil, after being captured by him to do his will." It is difficult to see from the perspective of others, to get inside their skin, and allow their experiences to inform our lives. Yet, these are necessary works for the Church moving forward.

What I am suggesting is primarily a change in tone from one of imposition to one of invitation, but each of us must pursue reconciliation, Agape, and a non-judgmental attitude *intentionally*. It means cooperation and true community without the dissolution of anyone's culture, personhood, or history, *including white people*. It is a fellowship based on the true Agape love of Christ and not a political subterfuge. DeGruchy calls the Body of Christ, ". . . a new humanity [of people] freed from dominating and exploiting others to be with and for others."[6] All of this rests on the understanding that we are members of God's kingdom, of the Kingdom of God. That is our objective reality. Daniel Clendenin writes, "Authentic Christian experience trusts in the power of the Holy Spirit to give our 'presence' a revolutionary and explosive force in history."[7]

―――

Digging deeper to one root of the matter, we confront the economic component. Consider 1 Timothy 6:5-11, KJV, ". . . perverse disputing of men of corrupt minds, and destitute of the truth, supposing that gain is godliness: from such withdraw thyself. But godliness with contentment is great gain. For we brought nothing into this world, and we can certainly carry nothing out. And having food and raiment let us be content therewith. But they that will be rich fall into temptation and a snare, and into many foolish and hurtful lusts, which drown men in destruction and perdition. For the love of money is [a] root of all [kinds of] evil: which while some have coveted after, they have erred from the faith and pierced themselves through with many sorrows. But thou, O man of God, flee these things . . ."

That we would heed these few words! What misery would be avoided! This is how God's people show themselves to the world. For "this present distress" in our nation would it not be too much to admonish every confessing Christian to downsize and de-accumulate, to work less, buy less, do less, be more, to become poor that we may become rich? Do we ascribe to the endemic belief that "rich" means someone else?

The atrocities committed against the Native Americans and the African slaves were committed out of a heart of deep spiritual sickness and for economic purposes. These actions were part of a tidal wave of human degradation and environmental destruction that continues to this very minute and affects every one of us regardless of our race or socio-economic status. From this, of necessity, developed a deep psychology of racial and class hatred. For the West, it has roots in Darwin, the Civil War, the Industrial Revolution, and, unfortunately, in the millennialist theology of the Protestant church.

I would like to add a caveat about racism and such. The powers that be have vested interests in keeping race relations strained and dysfunctional for a variety of reasons. Some of these, I believe, are spiritual. Many are good for politicians and "news" moguls. I see a lot more positive potential for good at the individual and community level when people refuse to play the game and instead seek real ways to integrate and build relationships. The Church is an ideal vehicle for this if we will have it, but we need "boots on the ground," people willing to meet with people over the long haul.

I would recommend Eugene McCarraher's "Enchantments of Mammon: How Capitalism Became the Religion of Modernity," which traces at great length, with extensive research, and painful erudition the physical and psychological subjugation of our nation to a destructive ethos of labor devoid of personal creativity, to a system of management and media designed to produce obedient workers at the cost of our minds, our bodies, and our freedom. All this is done with the help of a firmly entrenched "entertainment" industry and a consumerist ethic that keeps the general populace "satisfied" with their station in life. Our mental illness statistics would show that we are not satisfied at all. We are subdued and distracted. Aldous Huxley was prescient in writing "Brave New World."

It is not a matter of choosing between socialism/communism or capitalism, as so many of us so intractably maintain. Within the church, entertaining this false dichotomy makes us become political belligerents who drive people away from the house of God if anything. It is for lack of seeing other ways of being in the world. Our choice is between acting on the faithfulness of God in obedience to the gospel, and the tragedy of a life of fear, denial, and covetousness. See 1 John 2:15-17.

The illusions of these beliefs are compound, and the proliferation of these types of misdirected, politicized fears

On the Christian in the World

have wrought all manner of real devastation. An honest look back at the anti-Communist activities of the United States government, our disastrous meddling in foreign governments, proxy wars with Russia, the war in Viet Nam, and our wars in the oil-producing nations reveal many discomfiting realities that must be considered in the development of an honest Christian ethic. Likewise, many of us have refused to take a critical look at the American brand of capitalism. The largest companies are taking over an obscene amount of wealth and power in this nation. They are holding sway over our federal government. The gap between the wealthy and the poor is likewise obscene, and a nation that boasts of having abolished slavery has simply exported the bulk of its manufacturing to communist and third world nations, many with horrific records of human rights abuses. (I recently heard the "third world" described as not under-developed, but over-exploited. Would our terrifying amount of power be put to better use by helping stabilize the nations in our hemisphere, by helping them develop their manufacturing and industry, so they may enjoy the wealth of their nations, instead of using them as sources of raw materials and cheap labor? An oversimplification to be sure, but a point that is worth consideration. Our relationship with China could be the subject of many more books, but we would do well to not purchase anything made there when possible.)

Many Americans think nothing of the constant consumption of items made in China and developing nations. Soon we may have no choice! No American worker or labor union would tolerate the conditions endured by countless workers, slaves, and child laborers the world over who manufacture/process the food and products we buy with impunity. We continue to patronize the big box stores that are consuming our communities, turning them into a long, homogeneous economic vacuum, and we are content as long as the supply of "stuff" keeps coming. We celebrate it! It behooves the people of God to learn "how the sausage is made," and to face our reality. What we do, what we eat, where and how we spend our money hurts real people, hurts animals on a mass scale, and hurts our environment, God's property that we have been charged to steward. It is a common Christian understanding that we will give an account of our lives before God. See 2 Cor 5:10. Those hurt are not just *over there* somewhere. And, I believe our supply of stuff is dwindling and will continue to do so moving forward. Notice the shelves of your stores and the wait times on many ordered products in the wake of the Covid-19 pandemic. Those of us who are not ready with new psychology and a renewed trust in God will not be able to endure coming changes.

As stated before, there are many people we would consider to be "outside" the Body of Christ whose understanding of these things far outweighs ours, people who understand and appreciate the inherent goodness of the created order and our responsibility to steward it, who see the ravages of unbridled industrialization, endless warfare, and the dehumanizing culture of wantonness, wastefulness, and consumerism.

I challenge us to meet these "enemies" on the grounds of humility, understanding, and the admonitions of Scripture. See Rev 11:18, 18:13b, Rom 8:19-22, Jer 12:4, 10-11, James 5:1-6.

Further, on the question of capitalism versus socialism/communism, McCarraher puts forward that all of these systems are concerned solely with production for profit, in an ethos of scarcity (i.e., a society that keeps human beings in a constant state of anxiety about provision and dissatisfaction with what one currently has), the subjugation of the worker through the psychological splitting of the mind from the body, and lastly through the establishment of a managerial elite who will make the decisions. He goes on, "... American socialists accepted and even celebrated the corporate mechanization of communion ... [and] ... the authoritarian features of Soviet industry were modeled directly after the most imperious brand of *American* corporate discipline [the Taylor system]." (emphasis mine)[8]

As the seed, so the fruit.

Dorothy Sayers wrote that oppressive economic systems "... could not be kept up without the gluttony of the consumer. The point is that without any legislation whatever, the whole system would come crashing down in a day if every consumer were voluntarily to restrict purchases to the things really needed."[9] This is of course why there exists a madly funded advertising and entertainment industry, to keep us from the kind of contentment of life that might allow for a harmonious existence with each other and the planet, to prevent the equitable distribution of wealth, to keep us distracted enough to avoid honest reflection, and to persist in inaction. These systems are also set up to funnel the wealth and tax monies of the poor and the middle class to a very small number of people at the top of the pyramid.

In addition to the impulse to distraction and inaction, are the myths perpetuated by what we call the scientific community. James Kunstler in his book, *Living in the Long Emergency,* pulls no punches in outlining the "post-industrial decline" in which we now live. He paints a bleak picture of our fragile electrical grid (upon which depends all of the technology and entertainment we trust so much), the coming end of fossil fuels, and the unsustainability of so many of our "green" energy solutions. He calls out the "techno-narcissism and organizational grandiosity" of the tech industry, i.e., the idea that TECHNOLOGY, like some magic word, can solve every problem, and that knowing what a problem *is* is equivalent to solving it.[10] He does not suggest that the world is ending tomorrow, but that the world and our lives are changing and are going to change in major ways. This is happening now. For some contrary viewpoints, I may suggest *Drawdown, the most comprehensive plan ever proposed to reverse global warming,* edited by Paul Hawken, and *Factfulness: Ten Reasons We Are Wrong About the World—and Why Things Are Better Than You Think,* by Hans Rosling.

To further paint the historical picture, it should be understood by every Christian and every human being, that the spirit of mammon, or covetousness, affects us in every way. Let us look briefly at just one of many, many examples.

Only a few generations ago, most people lived on farms or in very small towns. They ate meats, dairy, fruits, and vegetables, much of which were grown near where they lived, if not on their property. While they being humans certainly faced ailments of various sorts, and while science and medicine continue to make incredible discoveries, we have to ask if our forebears faced the types and rates of cancer, obesity, hypertension, diabetes, auto-immune disorders, allergies, and myriad psychiatric disorders that we do now. We ask if what they put in their bodies even faintly resembles what we put in ours. We ask about the nature of their more-intact family and social structures compared to ours which have been obliterated, by many accounts due to the vacuity of Christian spiritual life after the world wars and occasioned by affluence. I would also like to leave a wide berth for and celebrate the champions of justice, knowledge, and gospel who have existed in every era, the labor leaders, the mental health pioneers, the scientists, the child advocates, the abolitionists, the social architects, and so on. While sin and injustice have always been around, God has always been present in his world.

Continuing, the powers that be decided that food should be mass-produced cheaply and commodified in the same manner as everything else. This one example of mechanization psychology unleashed a chain-reaction of devastating and far-reaching consequences, rooted firmly in economic avarice, the byproducts being untold human misery and environmental destruction. It spawned the multi-trillion dollar "food," "pharma," and "health" care disasters of our present undoing.

Because grains could be farmed and processed cheaply, preserved for a long time, and transported long distances, the industry turned to annual monocropping. Huge swaths of land were clear-cut, defoliated, and plowed. All animals were driven off, and in the case of necessary predatory animals, hunted into oblivion. A single crop would then be planted on the whole. Few people in our modern society understand the far-reaching consequences of this practice, and the psychology undergirding it. I certainly did not. I would suggest reading, as a start, Lierre Keith's "The Vegetarian Myth." It makes no pretense to moderation, but it contains in-depth information that we all need to understand. Let us remember that this is but an example of a larger societal sickness.

Annual monocropping causes a number of things to happen. (In our case these things happen on a mass scale. As of 2019, this amounts to over 897 million acres.[11] For reference, the state of Texas where I live is about 172 million acres of total land mass. There are at least forty million acres of lawns in the US as well, requiring an astounding amount of our diminishing water supply to maintain.) First, the obvious: trees, shrubs, and grassland are components of vital ecosystems, essential to the survival of myriad plants and animals, bees, birds, and mammals. And, by destroying predators, we upset a natural balance that allows the earth to work. With no predators, the ruminants, animals like deer, elk, antelope, and moose, will increase without restraint and be forced to compete for diminishing grasslands.

And *grass,* not wheat or any other grain, is arguably the real stuff of life.

The clearing of the ecosystem likewise destroys pollinating insects which are essential for survival and flourishing, not only of foodstuffs but of all sorts of flowers. We have not even mentioned yet the aesthetic of beauty! It is essential to understanding and spreading the gospel, and has been supplanted by utilitarianism, consumerism, and busyness. Consider the words of NT Wright, "The church, because it is the family that believes in hope for new creation, should be the place in every town and village where new creativity bursts forth for the whole community, pointing to the hope that, like all beauty, always comes as a surprise."[12] This type of gospel- promoting psychology is simply not possible when our *modus operandi* is the constant destruction of the existing creation, whether through active exploitation or passive complicity.

The topsoil itself is a complex entity composed of millions of plants, roots, molds, and microorganisms. It is the foundation of an ecosystem, an unimaginable symbiosis of flora and fauna. To simply rip all of this out is devastating.

On the Christian in the World

Over time, the plowed, single-crop land, with its microorganic substrate destroyed, will produce a disease-vulnerable crop from a base of diminishing nutritional content (remember that the living topsoil has been destroyed, and it no longer has a variety of flora to recycle every year). The soil becomes depleted of particular nutrients due to the needs of a single crop. And, since the diversity of insects and animals has been driven off, the crop becomes extremely vulnerable to pests and disease. For a single crop planted over a large area, all can be lost in an instant. From these practices stems the need for the constant use of commercial fertilizers, (many made from our diminishing fossil fuels. There are few if any, safe industrial options.) dangerous chemical pesticides, and the need to genetically modify our "foodstuffs." This creates toxic conditions for the earth, man, and beast alike.

Grains are then used to make feed for factory-farmed animals when they should be living on grass. Our factory farming practices then necessitate the use of more chemical additives. These and so many other foodstuffs are then heavily processed, crammed into every conceivable product on the shelves of your grocery store, and labeled "food." In addition to these ecological damages, the effects of the industrialization and commodification of the food supply are many and include the destruction of small farms and businesses, a unique complex of health problems, the use of great amounts of fossil fuels, plastics, and poisons, and the driving of people to urban centers, which brings its own set of problems to humanity.

This is to say nothing of the treatment of the animals we eat and from whom we get our eggs. We need to learn what many factory farms do with their waste as well, how these large operations destroy property values around them, and how aerosolized waste affects the people who live on the periphery.

There are race and class components involved as well since the periphery of industrial operations tends to be low-value homes, and low-income residents by default. We need to learn about how lobbying works at the state and federal levels. We need to understand that *very* few companies sell all of the "foods" you see in the grocery store, and how they operate here and in other countries.

One great sadness of all of this is that it is completely unnecessary. There are millions of pounds of nitrogen, for example, in the air above every acre of ground, accessible through natural processes. There are nearly limitless supplies of phosphorus and potassium available in the subsoil from natural sources. Crop rotations, green manures, composting, diversification, permaculture, *satoyama,* and ley farming (the rotation of vegetable-producing land to grazing land and back), are some examples of sustainable food production practices that can negate the need for chemical inputs. This knowledge has been available for hundreds of years but has been obscured since the late 1800s due to avarice. The *Industry* would rather sell toxic chemicals than allow for healthy food and community development. There seems to be no domain of human activity that does not operate under this toxic psychology.

Many people would protest in defense of industry that it creates jobs. As we speak, our community has "won" a distribution facility for a monolithic corporation. Jobs, jobs, jobs. Our town motto is "Wide Open Spaces and Endless Opportunities," as if economic development is the only metric for life, as if the bioregion were inconsequential, as if the infrastructure and crime problems we face are beside the point of unbridled development. Many of us have never been exposed to alternative models of community development or more equitable business models than the constant drive toward monopoly we experience in the US. This sad fact seems to be true for our civic leaders as well.

Eliot Coleman grows food at a commercial scale at his Four Season Farm *in Maine*, using crop rotation, green manures, natural soil amendments, and composts. He does not use commercial fertilizers. He does not use pesticides. He has several movable greenhouses, one minimally heated, that allow him to grow food all year, even at that latitude. Best practices, gleaned from agricultural wisdom that existed *before the Industrial Revolution*, university research travels abroad, and extensive experience has taught him the reality of healthy food production. See his book, *The New Organic Grower*, now in a 30th-anniversary edition. These are just a couple of examples of more holistic community development and agriculture models. See also the Lubbock Disparity Report in the recommended reading. Has our leadership been exposed to these models? Has the constituency pressed them for a buy-in to better ways of doing business? Does this matter to God and the gospel? I think so. It matters how we build our communities, and how we steward our resources. Integrity matters in government. Holism in development has an impact on crime and mental health, on the environment, on human engagement, and thus what a community *is* and does. The effect is additive.

To proceed, the very basic level of activism is to get educated, and then stop supporting destructive industries, destructive means of industry, and destructive psychologies in every way possible. The more we learn in this world "how the sausage is made," the more overwhelming and depressing it can seem, and our tale of "annual monocropping" is but one inadequate illustration of a principle. Please see the recommended reading at the end of this work, as many people have treated these subjects with much more skill and depth.

What can we do to begin in a real way? First, we must remember that we are God's kingdom people, living in a world that will only be fully redeemed at his appearing, but also that we each have a special mission to fulfill. That should give us hope inwardly, and hope to share with others. Our charge to stewardship and sanctification give us the impulse to move forward doing good in this world. We start where we are.

We can begin to withdraw support from harmful systems through a number of practices. It seems good to develop a new psychology of our consumption, one that promotes well-being for self, others, and the earth. Food that is grown organically/biologically within your local "bioregion" not only saves the world from that much fossil fuel and chemical usage, but supports local economies, a sense of community, and physical health. The rebuilding of local food systems is fertile ground (forgive the pun) for positive activism. We grow our minds and our communities as we grow and share our food. It is psychologically healing and satisfying. It builds community, and it often diverts water that would otherwise go exclusively to lawns. Go to farmers' markets. Find meat that is locally raised on pasture and humanely processed. There are alternatives to our mass-produced nightmare.

A garden in every yard! What in the world does this have to do with the Gospel?

One fitness guru puts it thus, "Eat meat and vegetables, nuts and seeds, some fruit, little starch, and no sugar."[13] I write that a bit tongue in cheek, but notice what is missing: all the packaged/processed products that make us sick. And make no mistake about it, we are sick. Remember also that a massive socialization campaign began several generations ago to convince and train people into believing that that box, bag, or can of chemicals is food. Our reality is also such that one cannot buy food or any other product without purchasing plastic, even our fruits and vegetables. This is a great sadness. The subjects of food, diet, factory farming, government lobbying, disease, healthcare, and insurance are endless and fraught with confusion, misinformation, and outright deception, but it behooves the Christian to learn to live more innocently and without reproach. This does connect to the proliferation of the gospel and the stewardship of God's creation. See Gen 1:26-28, 2:15, Mt 25:14f.

We consider some general principles. Every economic injustice is a human rights injustice. Every ecological injustice is a human rights injustice. (Even those of us who refuse to see the created order as anything other than *stuff* cannot deny this.) One of the most powerful things we can do as Christians is to be educated and intentional about where our money goes. If we take a minute to meditate on Isaiah chapter 58, and others that we have mentioned, we will see that God is concerned about issues of human justice. See also Micah 6:8.

Likewise, these issues have eschatological, gospel import. Many of us for various reasons have looked at the "social gospel" as a deviation from the real work of winning souls. While at times and on some levels this claim is legitimate, perhaps we have allowed our criticisms to drive us to inaction, or to a type of evangelism that robs human dignity rather than cultivates it. We will develop this holistic concept of the gospel as the work progresses.

Speaking from an eschatological perspective, let us consider once again the Genesis charge, the parable of the talents, the charge in Isaiah 58, and the word in 1 Corinthians 3:11-15 which states that our works in this life will be tried by fire. We are here to build abiding and valuable works upon the foundation of Jesus. See Ephesians 2:8-10; we were saved by grace and created for good works that God ordained for us long before we were even born. See the epistle of James and its emphasis on the meeting of basic needs, practical ethics, and community. See 1 Peter 2:15. The good deeds of the Christian are the witness of the Church to those who accuse us of evil. How terrible when the world has a basis to do so!

May your revolutionary impact take place *somewhere*! Let it be on your block, at work, in your community, or your nation. And please don't confuse it with the ethos of divisive politics, especially as we have wedded it to the Church. The body of Christ *must* re-evaluate and challenge her relationship with the political machine. Are the bitter signs and bumper stickers promoting the gospel, changing *anyone's* mind, or encouraging our faith in Christ? Are we aware of the profound effect constant (or even frequent) exposure to the mainstream media has on our minds? On the articulation of our professed faith and values? I submit through personal experience that even brief exposure to MSM after a time of abstaining causes instant anger and anxiety. A steady diet of it cannot but be a tragedy.

Many of us protest that we cannot just bury our heads in the sand when it comes to world events. This is difficult ground to be sure. It seems it would be worth it to seek out relevant news and to vet sources with severity. Then, it would be good to limit our exposure to media to that which is necessary for each of us in our milieu. There is a whole world at each of our fingertips, where God has placed us, that could use our unique contributions, love, presence, and activism. It seems that our time and energy would be better spent being kingdom citizens in our communities, rather than stewing in the overwhelming panic and outrage of the "news" industry.

Do we have more faith in Jesus Christ than in the political parties and the election cycles? This question bears a long reflection. The anxieties and fears that come with the political machinations of our country betray to many of us where our real trust lies. And if that be the case, what do we have to offer the wider world? The Christian's true influence is in our separateness, our prayers, and our Agape. If we are enmeshed with this present age, we are no longer a place for the lost to flee *to*!

I am convinced that the vast majority of our hardline political opinions are formed and entrenched through a mechanism that dehumanizes the "other." It is satanic in origin. This dehumanization is necessary because rational analysis of any social issue requires us to first recognize that it is far more complex than it appears. Understanding requires hard work, so human comfort and laziness can often get in the way, not to mention the sheer difficulty of wading through information overload and misinformation. See Prov 1:20, 2:3-4. Next, this dehumanization is necessary because to concede the humanity of the "other" is in its essence frightening. It means I must give up something. It means I may be taken advantage of. (And I certainly will, but is that the metric of Jesus?) To concede the humanity and status of the "other" is to acknowledge the unfairness of the status quo and my guilt in complicity. This is inherent in racism, classism, and all forms of discrimination. It is the hideous imputed psychology that has made all atrocity possible, whether in warfare, slavery and exploitation, or the quiet denial of the average citizen of the impact of our choices. It is also expressly addressed in Scripture. See Jas 2:1f, Acts 10:34, Rom 2:11, Eph 6:9, Col 3:25, 1 Pet 1:17. Galatians 3:26-29 tells us that the "putting on" of Christ has erased all discrimination based on race, nationality, class, and gender. I believe that in the spirit and ethos of Christ we would wish to see this same transformation take place for all people. It should be a distinguishing feature of the body of Christ, but it is obvious by looking in the parking lots of many churches and seeing the widespread proliferation of alternative "communities" and "villages" that this is not so.

To be fair, we must take into consideration the inherent offense of the gospel. Maintaining that objective reality means we are all sinners, living in a world that is under the just judgment of God, who has the authority to make an accounting of us, with a final and ultimate judgment yet to come will drive people away of its own merit. That is tragic, but it is not a fault of the Church. However, the Christian also carries within him or her the promise of human restoration, of reconciliation with God, who does indeed love us and desires mercy over judgment, eternal life, final justice, and renewal of the created order. This is a holistic rendering of the truth. It is something that the atheistic, or the humanistic world cannot offer, regardless of the apparent goodness or strength of their causes. It is also something that the compromised church cannot offer, contrary to all appearances. So, the American Church finds itself in the quandary of relearning how to live and speak the truth *in Love,* or in learning how to speak the truth at all!

One of the urgent and difficult tasks the Church faces in our modern hour is that of learning to engage our modern world with truth. It has been subsumed under illogical and belligerent ideologies, that will hear no reason, and it has erected massive structures to protect itself. We are in desperate need of prayer, wisdom, and much research.

My personal epiphanies came through some events over the past few years. I have endured great internal wrestling. So woven into our fabric is this need to be "better than," that only through the most intentional labor and the help of the Holy Spirit is it exorcised.

―――

In 2005, Hurricane Katrina blew through the south, devastating New Orleans especially. I was a brand new EMT riding the ambulance here in my hometown. At one point not long after the storm, several ambulances, buses, and a whole cadre of disaster response agencies were dispatched to the local airport. We made our way in. Tables were piled high with food and bottled water. Bus after bus arrived to pick up Katrina's refugees. They were mostly indigent. They were almost all African-American people. Many of them would stay right here in my hometown.

Meanwhile, thanks to endless wars the world over, and thanks to 9/11, many people were fleeing the developing world, the Middle East, and Africa, and heading for Europe, Scandinavia, the United States, and Canada. In short, there has been a mass migration of people to the West.

My hometown was hit especially hard. We went overnight from having four or five languages spoken regionally to around eighty. It is my understanding that one or two agencies are responsible for resettling people in our community, though I am open to correction.

In the 1970s there was the resettlement of people from

southeast Asia due to the Vietnam war. They landed mostly in the Northeast part of our city.

Being in Texas, we have a constant flow of Hispanic immigrants illegally crossing our southern border, a perennial and bitter issue that our governments refuse to address rationally.

This sudden influx of so many people from so many different cultures has been problematic. Many of them depend on government assistance, (whether they want it or not!) and so very many of them have displaced native workers in our ever-increasing number of Walmarts and in the beef packing plants. The education system here has been put under tremendous strain. We have been the subject of sociological studies and angry online videos. There are frequent meetings between our city officials and other agencies to adapt to the many changes taking place. At times we have had to ask for respite, being overwhelmed.

This is a situation that can breed fears, resentments, and communication problems. I ran a call late one night in which a young immigrant man drove his young female passenger through an intersection at a high rate of speed, into a tree and a large brick wall on the edge of a gated community. The passenger side of the vehicle was torn completely away in a mangled mass. The passenger was laying on the ground, unconscious. The driver was walked to a police car where he belligerently taunted every responder on the scene. I remember asking my officer to let the man out of the police car so I could beat him. Such was my anger at "them." We tried to save the girl, but we could not.

Our social services are strained. The poor who were already here are now pressed further by the increased need.

On the Christian in the World

Our homeless population has exploded here, keeping pace, I think, with our rapid urbanization. Our city government, meanwhile, has seemed to put the bulk of its efforts into a massive downtown revitalization project. As I write, they are asking for 275 million dollars to renovate our convention center. They are also holding meetings to close city parks, or selling them to commercial developers, displaying a profound misunderstanding of what a community should be. (In an update, the convention center proposal was voted down).

Urbanization and residential development continue at a breakneck pace. Our population is exploding. People and large industries who have no stake in our community or people beyond economic gain are flooding into Texas from the unsustainable nightmares on the coasts, often at the behest of our economic development corporation. For the moment there are jobs, industries, and affordable homes (thousands of which are being built every day, it seems!). It feels to me as if we are being swallowed up by a flood against which we have no defense.

Although this may seem like a digression, I believe it helps paint a picture. In education, healthcare, emergency services, social services, community development, and employment, the atmosphere is ripe for anger. Cultural dysphoria and dissonance develop during stressful encounters and wherever money, resources, and services are involved. There are often resentments toward newly arrived African immigrants from resident African-Americans. This is a deep issue that requires much study, but it is very real.

I feel the anger, the resentment, and the frustration at a world and a community that has changed so much, in so little time, and without my permission. I am angry at the NGOs and the politicians who have done these things. There are often political and economic angles to these issues that are infuriating.

A steady influx of cheap labor and an absolute refusal of our governments to remedy our border crisis panders to the corrupt on both "sides of the aisle." I am angry at the greedy, unbridled expansion, and the apparent disconnect of our city government in so many aspects of planning. More houses. More businesses. The bottom line is the bottom line. Forget about parks. Forget about making our communities walkable, scalable, and mixed-use, as I've heard it said, just keep building.

My intention here is full disclosure. It is fair to say that this world is grossly imperfect. I have attempted to present, in brief, the reality of the frustration felt by myself and many other people, right or wrong, just or unjust.

The following should help set the stage for how we are engaging some of these frustrations. A few years ago my family and I were in the midst of some difficult personal issues. In addition, I had through much pain, shame, and guilt, given up on the church we had attended for almost a decade. I will not get into the "why's" here. I began visiting other churches, usually alone. Having been enamored with Martin Luther before and during a brief stint at Denver Seminary, I decided to visit a Lutheran church. I went for a while, comforted by the liturgy and the elevated status of the Lord's supper. I met with the pastor a couple of times. Although a few people were certainly kind, the overall feel of the place was quite cold. Many of the laity seemed to be unconcerned and even put off by the presence of new people. The thrust of the ministry often seemed to be disproving the teachings of other denominations, writers, and pastors. Another Lutheran church we visited once felt even colder.

We tried a Baptist church. The laity were very kind to us. We thought we might have found a good spot. I had initially been attracted to this place after attending a friend's baptism there and hearing the gospel message preached by the pastor. I believe he is a good man. However, it soon became apparent that some dynamics in the leadership, and interactions we had with them at the outset, were going to make this church untenable for us.

We tried another Baptist church closer to our home. We got into a Sunday school class. My kids tried the youth and never meshed. My younger daughter kept going to our old church youth group. My older daughter tried a couple of groups without success. She felt, by this time, quite wounded at the hands of the youth in the church.

I am not leveling criticism at any particular denominations, or even non-denominations, just describing our own unique experiences.

This period, as painful as it was, led to the births of at least two life-changing phenomena that I believe were orchestrated by God. I will elaborate further as we go, but the events were these: my wife got involved in teaching English as a Second Language (ESL) through this church, and through the Sunday school class we met a couple who were on the verge of starting a home church.

My wife fell in love with the ESL ministry. She frequently regaled me with tales of her students, their lives and struggles, and funny anecdotes. Some of her favorites were the Somali ladies and the ladies from Myanmar, and an elderly *gentle*man named Sami who was hard of hearing and often interrupted the class. One Mexican man had been here many years and spoke English well, but continued coming to class to meet with his beloved friends.

As she shared stories of her experiences in ESL, my resentments and fears were provoked. My well-rehearsed vitriol against the politicians, the NGOs, and the aggravating "them" that we dealt with at work boiled to the surface.

While all of this was going on, I began to feel the same sense of suffocation and futility sitting in services at this new church.

I broke that news to my wife and once again we were fractured. Our children's hearts were broken.

My younger daughter continued to attend youth functions at our old church. We would show up for choir concerts and holiday stuff. My older daughter tried a youth group at one of the large Presbyterian churches and felt the same sense of indifference and rejection she felt at our old church, and our current one. She was withdrawing and in great pain. She went through a phase of cutting herself.

Our new friends in Sunday school had meanwhile been praying over the idea of a home church. At first, they had wanted to create a small and intimate venue where they might invite and build relationships with people who had either been "de-churched," or who would not darken the doors of a church in the first place. They would talk together, and eat together. The plan at the time was to funnel these folks into the church after a significant number of relationships had been established. When they brought this idea to their church leadership, they were informed that the church was not interested. I do not know any other details of this event, so I cannot speak about it.

In the meantime, I began having coffee and talking with the husband of this couple. He extended the invitation to visit the home church with no pressure. I told him that it sounded interesting and that I would like to check it out sometime.

It was during this period that God began to work on my heart.

I began to realize the incongruence between fear and anger, and the Spirit of Christ. I started to see a separation between the sometimes dubious or short-sighted activities of NGOs, politicians, and opportunists, versus the face of an individual, created in the image and likeness of God, no matter where they are from, how they got here, or their station in life. God began to *re-humanize* the "other" in my heart. This process is taking place in a surprising number of ways.

I have begun to consider the fundamental needs of a human being, each of whom requires an incredible number of resources to flourish. Even at a primitive level (and I would contend that a primitive level might be the height of human flourishing) a single human being needs food, clothing, and shelter daily. We need medical and dental care. We need love, acceptance, and community. We need meaning. We need a sense of safety and an adequate, functioning, internal locus of control. Something clicked in me leaving the dentist one day after having a painful tooth worked on. How demoralizing would it be for a human being not to have access to basic goods, services, and medical care. How would it feel to live in constant uncertainty regarding rudimentary needs, not to mention the devastation wrought by a major illness, injury, or surgery? This is the reality for countless Americans already. Even the well-off could be financially ruined under our current system by such an event. How much more for displaced refugees living with war trauma? It is also a fair question to consider how much of the rest of the world we can support when we are already trillions of dollars in debt as a nation, and will not provide affordable and adequate healthcare for our own citizens. Again, no easy answers.

Further, because of my job and certain life experiences, I've been treated for PTSD, depression, and anxiety. My job as a firefighter provides me with yearly physicals, and a clinic I can use at no additional cost to me. I do not say free because *everything* is paid for by someone. We would do well to remember that. Continuing, my job provides me with income, time off for vacations, and a pension. I cannot imagine not having access to physical and mental health care, time off, familiarity, to a reasonable expectation of safety. I began to consider the plight of people who have difficulty accessing these things, and compare that to some of my internal prejudices and resentments. In the light of my profession of Jesus Christ, I would have to change. I would reiterate that these difficulties are also the case for many American citizens already.

I accepted my wife's invitation to help teach ESL classes. We took the orientation classes where language teaching methods and cultural issues were discussed. We learned a bit about what kinds of physical contact or mannerisms could be construed as offensive or inappropriate. Amusing or tragic anecdotes were shared about people with unfamiliar names. Without a doubt, the fears and frustrations reared their heads, but I persisted.

We got our teaching materials together. We made a lesson plan. We prayed. My wife was giddy with anticipation. She has fallen head over heels in love with these people.

The first day of class arrived down in the sprawling, labyrinthine basement of the Baptist church. This ministry has been extant for over fifty years. The halls filled to bursting with students. I saw burkhas and scarves and sandals. I saw people of all hues of black and brown. I smelled spices, body odors, and perfumes. I heard a cacophony of speech and laughing. Ladies were holding hands in familial custom. There was no order to the sauntering crowd, no traffic lanes. We had been warned to kiss being in a hurry goodbye. Much of the rest of the world does not put near the emphasis on the clock that we do. It may be good medicine for some of us.

Over the first twenty minutes or so of scheduled class time, our students filtered in. For many of these people who work long hours at meat-packing plants, or elsewhere, for women whose husbands often leave them for long periods driving trucks, whatever their circumstances, this time is often one of few opportunities to engage with loving friends and put aside the frightening and perhaps stifling isolation they may face in their new "home." One additional irony is that ESL class can be a time for the students to speak their native languages with friends.

My students came from Iran, Iraq, Sudan, South Sudan, Egypt, Somalia, Myanmar, Laos, and Mexico. Combined with all the other classes, it seemed we had over forty nations represented. I began to hear some of their stories. Many of them had fled wars and political violence. Many of them work long, grueling hours in the beef packing plants. All of them now live in an unfamiliar place, separated from family, friends, and familiarity by oceans. For me, this was the first time interacting with international people outside of the emergency setting.

Part of the ESL ministry involved visiting our students in their homes. This has been illuminating, to say the least, and a journey outside my comfort zone. I have sat on the floor of a couple of Muslim Somali homes to a feast of goat, chicken, rice, potatoes, flatbreads, and some things I cannot identify. We have been fed heaps of Asian foods, Mexican foods, and Middle Eastern foods. My wife has set up big parties for the students and the attendance has been enthusiastic. Our home church family hosted at least one of these gatherings in their home. I spent one night doubled over in horrific abdominal pain after a meal of unfamiliar foods.

I began to see how central the sharing of meals was to the community. I began to see the nucleus of God's intention. Is it not a feast (a wedding feast to be precise) that will mark the eschatological consummation of God's plan concerning his creation? In the bringing together of disparate and sometimes disconnected people who are strangers in a strange land, do we not approach the intention of God? Psalm 68:6 declares, "He setteth the solitary in families" (KJV). We consider Cana, the Lord's Supper, and so many other meals mentioned in the Scripture.

Another thing I began to notice was the extreme respect so many of these folks paid to us as "teachers." It has been humbling. I do not wish to paint all people as angels or to overlook social, religious, political, and cultural difficulties, but in the case of our students, I have found them to be kind and respectful people almost without exception. Also, as I have engaged in this ministry, I feel closer to what may be the true essence of Christianity.

I began to realize the untenability of my fears and resentments in light of my profession of Christ. I was able to begin separating my rantings and ravings against governments and NGOs from the faces of the individuals I was getting to know. I do not wish to diminish those grievances, because we as a society *do* have to face many uncomfortable realities. Again, how many people can a nation that is tens of *trillions* of dollars in debt support? Is it righteous to move entire people groups into communities without the approval and permission of the constituency our elected officials have sworn to represent? What do we owe *first* to native Americans, to Hispanic immigrants, who are our near neighbors, and some of the original inhabitants of this land as well? What do we owe to the citizens of the United States? We tend to nullify the culture and rights of US citizens, perhaps because so many are white. Our southern border is a warzone right now. Many of the *American* lakes, rivers, and towns in south Texas are uninhabitable for violence. Why are we not fixing this problem? And why, at the same time, are we moving so many people here from so many nations? There are endless relevant questions that are being bulldozed and written out of conscience in the rush to just get more people here. Many times, hard questions are shouted down as hateful rhetoric because we as a society are so polarized and incapable of deep, reflective dialogue. I have to turn the government and the institutions over to God as well and understand that war and the crises it brings are never convenient.

 Despite all of these grievances, I consider that I have Bibles on top of Bibles in my house. I could use them for coasters, but many of these people may have no other Bible, no other Jesus than me, standing in front of them. I could maintain my indignant, political fear and anger, and there is a time, place, and manner for appropriate political activism, but if I am a confessing Christian, I must learn to humanize the "other." I attempt through prayer, patience, and presence to eradicate discrimination and respect of persons from my heart. I still need God's help.

 Further, this mindset extends far beyond immigrants and

refugees only. The admonition is to heed the Scripture which states, "There is neither Greek nor Jew, there is neither bond nor free, there is neither male nor female: for ye are all one in Christ Jesus" (Gal 3:28, KJV). Regardless of race, nationality, socioeconomic status, gender, and even so many of the things we find distasteful or sinful, regardless of whether a person is within or without the body of Christ, we are to treat each person as they are, created in the image of God, who causes it to rain on all of us. See Mt 5:44-45, 9:9-13.

This mass migration of people, our post-industrial decline, and our bitterly polarized political scene all mean the potential for anger. We must not write off or demonize white people any more than any other group of people. We must not invalidate their grievances. As a Church, we must cultivate the unity of the Spirit among all people. See Eph 4:1-6.

I would again like to differentiate the Christian practice of Agape and the erasure of discrimination, from the progressive cultural-political movements of our day. While many of the stated ends of each framework may appear similar, nothing could be further from the truth. The former, in its purest essence, is the calling of human beings to repentance from sin, and faith in God. See Heb 6:1-2. It is the expression of the truth of the human condition, that we are indeed all sinners in need of a Savior, and that the world sits under the judgment of a just God. It is the renewal of hope for reconciliation with God and our fellows, hope for the world that is, and hope for the restoration of all things under Christ. See Romans 3:23, 5:8, 6:23, 8:1, 10:9, the "Romans Road" scriptures. Within this we find the highest value conferred upon humanity and the created order, and the possibility of true justice for all the oppressed, even though a renewal of thought and practice is needed in the Church like never before. See Ps 103:6, Rom 8:22, Rev 21:5.

The latter, in its purest essence, is a frightening redefinition of God as love without definite authority or moral imperative, and the confusing redefinition of human beings and functional human societies contrary to biology, science, and long-standing sociology. It is the imposition of severe limits of speech, thought, and action by those who claim to be championing freedom, love, and equality. It is the subsuming of corporate America and the entertainment industry, and the institutional suppression, dumbing-down, and punishment of those with dissenting views. It is most tragic that a significant part of the Western Church has also been subsumed under this cultural movement, and it will culminate in oppressive totalitarianism, even for its adherents, as it always has. Again, see Rev 18:4. See Hannah Arendt's, *The Origins of Totalitarianism*. Likewise, many of us have read George Orwell's *1984*, but few of us realize that we are living it right now. As a Christian, however, I must remember to treat others in the spirit of Christ, even when I disagree with their ideology. If we are subversive in any way, let it be in the sharing of truth and practical Agape love, leaving no grounds for accusations of hatred.

I have written this last bit at length in the hope that sharing some of my stories may help others who are struggling with anger, prejudice, and our changing landscape. It is essential to a much-needed paradigm shift among many of us. Brennan Manning writes, "Jesus deals the death blow to any distinction between the elite and the ordinary in Christian community."[14] I must confess again and again the temptation to fear and anger, to insularity, and the echo chamber.

To finish this section, I will suggest Derrick Jensen's, "The

Culture of Make Believe." Although there are without doubt other books along the same vein, this one does a remarkable job at articulating the psychology of hatred within Western culture, and it is not all about what we might consider extremism. It deftly and at length gets at the heart of all that I have but touched on. I considered not including it, as it is quite disturbing in many parts, but it would behoove all of God's people to pass through the fires of knowledge so we may see clearly. See also Alexander Solzhenitsyn's *Gulag Archipelago* for further reading on the development of harmful ideology. See Rod Dreher's *Live Not by Lies* for a more encapsulated discussion of our current moral crisis and imperative. Some of it may seem to be extreme material, but most of us do not understand the gravity of our spiritual situation and the spiritual forces arrayed against us. We are the proverbial frogs in the saucepot, and things are way worse than we know. Again, I am not advocating wallowing in morbidity, but until we attain an objective understanding of our world, and despair of its systems, we cannot appreciate the hope we have to offer in Christ. We cannot fully throw ourselves on the mercy and power of God, that we may be about his business, and be the revolutionary force he intends. Last, we will not be able to endure the coming difficulties.

4

CREATION CARE AND STEWARDSHIP

We have spoken in brief and the occasional anecdote about "mammon," human dignity, and the principle that every economic injustice is a human rights injustice. Expanding on this theme, we will now turn toward the created order. At this point, there is a confluence of powers spiritual, environmental, political, and social. We have already discussed the spiritual aspect. We will take a closer look at the political machine later, but now we must learn about the deep and surprising relevancy of the creation in God's plan, and in the machinations of this "world" (as convention) which the apostle John says, "Lies in wickedness" (1 John 5:19). It is essential for every Christian, and the Church as an institution to understand these dynamics so that we, as individuals and bodies, can begin to orient ourselves for the work of God's glory and gospel, for righteousness, responsible stewardship, justice, and the alleviation of suffering, to name just a few.

Laura Walls writes of Henry David Thoreau, who lived

A Christian Ethic for the Modern Church

in the early to mid-1800s, "Thoreau was a haunted man. He and everyone he knew was implicated: the evil of slavery, the damnation of the Indian, the global traffic in animal parts, the debasement of nature, the enclosure of the ancient commons[i.e.-that which was shared by the community for all manner of use, before the notion of private property helped propel the modern world into classism, competition, and want]—the threads of the modern global economy were spinning him and everyone around him into a dehumanizing web of destruction."[1] We could extend the list indefinitely. She further describes Thoreau's "conviction that attention to the natural environment confronted the root of all political evil."[2] Let us add this statement from Craig Sloane, "Christian martyrdom always has political overtones to it because it is where the kingdom of God and the kingdoms of this world collide."[3]

If we (rightly) set up the kingdom of God and the kingdoms, structures, and institutions of this world that "lies in wickedness," face to face, we may then draw certain illustrative conclusions. God indeed established order and authority. See the creation account in Genesis. See Romans chapter 13. God undoubtedly gave humanity authority over his creation, and what was intended to be a role as co-regents with God was wrecked when sin entered the world. Sin is the origin. It is this fact that sets the gospel apart from all other human beliefs, understanding, and endeavors. God also commissioned labor and the use of the earth's resources. See Deut 5:13, chapter 8, Ex 20:9, 23:12, 34:21. Likewise, God commanded a Sabbath. God, who is omnipotent, observed a Sabbath rest after creating our universe, not because he was tired, but because in his infinite wisdom and understanding, he knew that it was good and right. This principle is devastating in its implications. The disregarding of this simple command from God is indicative of human mistrust of God's objective goodness and his willingness and ability to provide. It is the inability to rest and enjoy all that God and we create. It is the spirit that breeds fear of lack in the human heart. Through myriad manifestations, we then try to provide for ourselves in the refusal of God's promised provision and care, and the boundaries of authority that would preserve love and equity among human beings. I contend that this is one of the deepest roots of human exploitation and misery, the fear of lack. This mindset leads to inner spiritual darkness that elevates the acquisition of capital to supreme status which then, by extension, causes all else to be secondary. This *all else* includes ALL ELSE: human beings, relationships, the earth's resources, and one's very self. As Jesus said, "You *cannot* serve God and mammon" (Mt 6:24, NKJV, emphasis mine). Without God, it is necessary to dominate through violence and oppression whether we are discussing nations, companies, families, or churches. We do what we have to do to survive.

I contend that the institution of the Sabbath is the foundation for all ethics. I believe this is borne out explicitly throughout the Hebrew testament, although this contention would require an exhaustive development that is partially expounded in separate essays. Let us, however, hit a few main points.

At its highest expression, the Sabbath is God's command to trust him completely for everything necessary to life and flourishing. It is his admonition to rest, to observe and enjoy him, his creation, our human relationships, and the work of one's hands. It is in this realm of observance that the seeds of art, music, beauty and the full spectrum of human flourishing exist. It is to be understood as the unity of the *imago Dei* in

A Christian Ethic for the Modern Church

the human being along with the creative capacity and process. These are the things that are so violently destroyed through industrialization, war, unbridled expansion, the utilitarian development of our communities, and the misery of our harried lives.

The Sabbath is the foundation of the equitable distribution of wealth. It is the basis for the ethical treatment of animals. God cares for the sparrow, he commands rest for animals within his Sabbath commandment. He states in Proverbs 12:10, "The righteous man cares for the needs of his animal." He pronounces judgment on those who "destroy the earth"(Rev 11:8).

Again, there is not space to address every grief. I will provide a recommended reading list at the end of this work. Do a web search on the Sixth Extinction. Research the effects of human industry on this earth, the application of toxic chemicals and the disposal of waste, the "food" industry, the "Medical Industrial Complex," the pharmaceutical industry, and industrial agriculture. The "healthcare" industry in the United States has a lobbying budget *four times* that of the defense industry.[4] That should raise some red flags!

We have destroyed ecosystems through rapacious deforestation and damaging methods of agriculture, fishing, mining, relentless chemical application, urbanization, and unbridled expansion instead of the measured development of, "... compact, walkable, mixed-use, human-scaled towns and neighborhoods."[5] Thoreau wondered at the fact that while he looked at nature and the forests as living sanctuaries of goodness, others only saw the board-foot value of the wood. Please read Walden and other suggested works on the creation if you have not. While Walden does expose the spiritual sickness of society, it is the counterpart to Jensen's

Creation Care and Stewardship

work in that it so deeply illuminates the positive side and spiritual depth and appreciation of the created order. Annie Dillard's *A Pilgrim at Tinker Creek* is a tale in a similar vein, showing us that there is so much more to *see!*

Closer to home are the personal lifestyles many of us have never analyzed or confronted. Luke 12:13-21 records the parable of the "bigger barns." Jesus said plainly, "Take care, and be on your guard against all covetousness, for one's life does not consist in the abundance of his possessions" (v15). The self-storage industry raked in 39.5 billion dollars in 2019.[6] These are the bigger barns.

As a Christian, am I content with food and clothing? Do I with impunity produce a constant stream of single-use plastic bags, cups, straws, and packaging? Have I considered the "Reduce, Reuse, Recycle" ethos? Have I considered sustainability measures such as composting in my production of food waste? Do I know where my money goes, who made the products I buy, and what conditions they work in? Do I understand the cost of human and animal suffering and of ecological damage incurred by what I buy, eat, drive, and wear, the house I live in, and where I shop?

We may also protest that industry does a far greater amount of environmental damage than my fast food waste, or whatever. However, I would submit again with Dorothy Sayers that those industries exist because of the aggregate of individual consumers. This is the psychological disconnect for us humans, the incorporation or personification of INDUSTRY. This allows us to create plausible deniability of sorts. *They* are destroying the environment. Whether we are discussing deforestation, unbridled development, or any other destructive practice, we escape responsibility by pointing *over there*. Our answer as the body of Christ must be collective action in the form of prayer and a refusal to continue consuming in harmful ways. For the Christian, it means a re-examination of life's priorities and the commands of Christ. We remember to view these thoughts and actions with a broad lens, knowing that responsible stewardship of the created order equals an increase in justice for oppressed people. It means the alleviation of suffering for people and living creatures. It means the preservation and promotion of the created order and its beauty which embodies the spirit of God's Sabbath. It means the development of a healthy personal psychology and recovery from the spirit of this age so that we are free for a life of loving action. In all of this, we are setting the stage for the goodness of the Gospel message.

We ask the question posed by Henry Thoreau, "Do I live innocently enough?" We as Christians must also do this in the context of the Word of God which says, "Love works no ill to his neighbor" (Rom 13:10). I will discuss the concept of the holistic gospel in the last section while outlining an ethical proposition that seems in harmony with the gospel of Jesus and the nature of God. First, though, we must take a brief look at one more of our most vexing difficulties.

5
CHRISTIANITY, THE POLITICAL APPARATUS, AND THE MEDIA

I can think of no more desperate need than for the Church and Christians to reform our involvement with the political apparatus and the mainstream media at a fundamental level. So deep-seated are the notions that the litmus test of our faith (and the faith, and even the human value of others!) is our political affiliation, that the kingdom of God and Christian activism consist in the legislation of sexual mores, and that God has placed an imperative upon his people to attain control over the institutions of this world. This is a distortion of the Gospel charge. We place such supreme weight on election cycles and who is in the White House that there is little chance of appealing to reason. It is tragic to go into church parking lots and see vitriolic political bumper stickers, knowing how bitter and divisive these things can be, while Jesus is pleading for us to go into the highways and the hedges and *compel them to come in*!

A Christian Ethic for the Modern Church

I am saddened to see presidents of Christian schools and well-known Christian leaders campaigning publicly for political candidates, and doing unbelievable mental and rhetorical gymnastics to paint them as people of the Christian faith, knowing the profound influence they have on their audiences. This dynamic is not lost on the political machine. Would our church leaders not better serve the kingdom of God by putting the boots of every Christian on the ground to love, feed, clothe, house, teach, and adopt one another into living communities, instead of promoting political rhetoric and consumer church? To deconstruct this mindset will be the work of generations if we have that much time before the return of Christ. Nevertheless, it must move forward with the utmost desperation. My personal experiences are mostly centered in the "Bible belt," although I have lived for brief periods on both coasts. I am not as well studied in the political and spiritual workings outside of the Protestant church, or among the "left," but I believe that a few general principles and observations will be salutary for all of the Church.

Doubtless, nothing is as painful as challenging our most deeply held beliefs. Most, or all of us do not even realize how automatic they are. Francis Schaeffer observes, "People have presuppositions, and they will live more consistently based on these presuppositions than even they may realize."[1] We are shaped by our environment, our genetics, our family of origin, and our life experiences. We learn to live and survive, to make sense of the world and our existence, to ensure that our needs are met. We develop a personal moral framework, which is our spiritual battleground. The idea of "personal truths" and systems of belief is thrust into the spotlight. The reality is that many of our psychological frameworks would not hold up to even the most rudimentary challenges. Perhaps that is why we hold to them with such violence.

We learn through experience and observation, through school and religious training, and a very powerful and deliberately engineered media complex. Whether branded "news," "entertainment," or "advertising," the media exists solely to shape your thinking and control your emotions, to keep you distracted, all while taking your money. What is most ironic is the fact that the advertising machine keeps us unsatisfied so we will keep buying what they are selling, while the entertainment industry carefully channels what should be our righteous anger at the state of the world around us into the vicarious glamour and violence of the screen. This prevents many people from lives of meaningful action and endeavor. I doubt many of us on our deathbeds will wish we had watched more TV or spent more time browsing useless content on the internet.

Even the most diligent parents and spiritual teachers find themselves eclipsed by the relentless and indefatigable torrent of data coming into our young people's lives (and our own) through the TV, the radio, and the endless scrollable junk food of the internet.

The major news networks are a cacophony of information overload, tickers, alerts, boxes in boxes endlessly repeating, and repetition is the mechanism by which ideologies are imprinted in the human mind. The product they are peddling is outrage, and we are addicted to it.

Author Randall Balmer challenges us to juxtapose Jesus' "Sermon on the Mount" with the political discourse of the religious right. I would encourage all of us to step back and observe these news outlets objectively, just before turning them off forever. Where is civil discourse? Where is corporate

A Christian Ethic for the Modern Church

responsibility? Corporate accountability! There is an amusing concept. Where is educated and unbiased information? We owe it to ourselves to learn just what the media *is*, so that we may live in truth and real freedom. The unfortunate fact is that many of us will choose the delusion because it seems easier at the moment.

Likewise, the battle for our morality, social engineering, and the subjugation of the citizen take place on the phone, computer, television, and movie screen. (The public school and grotesquely expensive university systems are likewise culpable). How much life has been extracted from each of us through these devices! It is especially tragic for the Christian person, who is the light of the world, to have wasted so many of the few and precious hours we have been given consuming banal, useless, deceptive, and harmful propaganda. Do the sermons we listen to or the Scriptures we read intersect our lives in any meaningful way? Do we receive it in any quantity sufficient to overcome the flood of worldly, engineered input we consume? Jaque Ellul laments, "The whole of civilization is designed to distract, thus man [kind] swallows whatever the media feeds. Man is profoundly incapable of meditation and reflection."[2] This ought not to be so.

Let us connect a major thread in this web. "In 2019, the total lobbying spending amounted to 3.47 billion US dollars."[3] This does not include the power *inherent* in the for-profit medical industry, the military-industrial complex, big food, big ag, big pharma, privatized prisons, the big box stores, tech monopolies, and the conflicts of interest between our bloated government oversight agencies and the corporate interest. When I talk about inherent power, I refer to the unassailable nature of these institutions. No one in power can be held accountable. I submit that our government has in great measure abdicated its responsibility to represent its constituency. It now exists to protect itself and the interests of the big corporate players. I will not be convinced otherwise until the end of corporate lobbying, severe limits on campaign contributions, and term limits for federal elected officials. I will not be convinced as long as our federal government refuses to solve our southern border crisis; until they address the environmental and human devastation perpetrated by our industries both here and abroad; until they address the monopolistic companies that are relentlessly driving the wealth of our nation into the hands of one percent of its citizens. Follow the money. Everything points back to this unholy marriage: the distraction of the entertainment industry, the advertising industry and its manufacture of needs, endless wars in the Middle East, and the "contrived and obsessive moral panic over race and sexual relations."[4] (ie-social justice causes foisted upon the populace by the media as a distraction from the conduct of our government and industries.) Further, the obscene costs of healthcare, the unnavigable labyrinth of health insurance, the exporting of manufacturing and service overseas, the staggering amount of invasive data collection and monitoring by the government and monolithic companies, the continuous acquisition of power during every national crisis, the tragic inefficiency of our legislative sessions, the insane incarceration rate of an allegedly developed and affluent nation. All of these things mean more money and power to the federal government and the big companies, and when the wheels of justice turn slowly, there is no justice. The COVID-19 pandemic is giving us a taste of that as the largest companies are getting richer while the rest of the nation is losing money, and small businesses are dying by the thousands. Perhaps all the fanfare surrounding the federal elections is aught but the little game they give us so we have a sense of personal influence and responsibility, lest we devolve into a true awareness.

We as the Church must realize that these worldly systems are under the sway of evil despite the preserving influence of God's saints the world over, and the psychology within the Church that suggests we need to control these institutions represents a departure from the gospel and the intention of God. We need to stop placing our hope and trust in these institutions and seek to be faithful witnesses within them when our situation dictates. To be sure, God tells his people to submit to the ordinance of man, to be law-abiding citizens, but we have so much more to offer this world. We must be clothed once again with the Spirit and intention of God, with the eschatological hope afforded us by the ministry of Jesus' life, death, and resurrection, by his ascension and glorification, by the promise of his return, and the consummation of this age. He will judge the earth, eradicate evil, and redeem and glorify his entire creation, including our bodies. God has a larger purpose.

The mission of controlling or repairing the systems of this world is antithetical to the gospel in the manner that so many of God's people are engaged in it now. Yet, inevitably, we must collide and/or work within these systems. Scripture and history are rife with good examples for us to follow: Joseph, Moses, Daniel, Jesus, Paul, William Wilberforce, Martin Luther King Jr, and the modern abolitionists who work to eradicate human trafficking in the forms of sex slavery, child labor, and soldiering, all of which involve cruelty and the destruction of human beings, and money and power just as we have discussed. I hope I have piqued your interest enough with this minute survey to do your research. Again, I will add a suggested reading list at the end of the book. So much of our worldview is, unfortunately, based on sentiment, socialization, denial, misinformation, and outright manipulation by powers spiritual, political, and corporate, that only through tremendous and deliberate labor, and often through grievous disillusionment is it possible to begin to see things as they are.

I intend to lay out a practical and workable ethic for the consideration of God's people, but first, we must look at the American church as an institution.

6
ON THE INSTITUTION OF CHURCH IN AMERICA

In apparent contradiction to the title of this section, it would be redundant to write a history of the church in America. Voluminous works exist to that end. I have just finished *Protestantism in America*, by Randall Balmer and Lauren F Winner. I would heartily recommend it. Other works such as *The Color of Compromise*, by Jemar Tisby, highlight the historical complexities of church and race, and how the Church might increase understanding and change for the better. I have read works that seem to have been conceived and promoted out of a wounded spirit and made irrational suggestions for change. National histories have always been religious and political battlegrounds, so it requires high levels of discernment, sifting, and *high levels of internal honesty* to separate fact from fiction and construct a balanced narrative. In addition, there are works written outside of what we would call history or theology which nevertheless have profound relevance for the body of Christ. Works already mentioned such as *Walden*, by Henry

A Christian Ethic for the Modern Church

Thoreau, Lierre Kieth's, *The Vegetarian Myth*, and *A Culture of Make Believe,* by Derek Jensen, are works of modern philosophy and social critique that compel us to challenge long-held beliefs and practices in the interest of personal wholeness and societal healing. While not everything is the gospel, wisdom can be found in many places. It behooves us to see where people are getting it right, no matter who they are.

This section will contain a fair amount of anecdote. I hope that by sharing my experience *in, with, and under* the Church, I might highlight a few of the issues facing us corporately, and perhaps give articulation to some of the internal dissonances many people are now feeling in their pews, couches, 501.3c's, or behind their lawnmowers on a Sunday.

I first believe that God is sovereign and that he will prepare and marry his bride, the Church, at the consummation of this age, whenever that is. In other words, he will ensure by his grace, a saved and sanctified community of believers. God loves his people. Further, not everyone in the church is a friend of the Church. As the apostle Paul said, "I know that after my departure fierce wolves will come in among you, not sparing the flock; and from among your own selves will arise men speaking twisted things, to draw away the disciples after them" (Acts 20:29-30). He tells us in Matthew 13 that it is the mysterious will of the Father to let the wheat and the tares grow together until the end. Further still, Scripture bears out from start to finish that God is always calling his people, whether they be the Israelites or the Church universal, back to himself. Consider the letters to the churches recorded in Revelation chapters two and three. Jesus himself, who is the head of the Church, praises, exhorts and rebukes his people unto repentance and perfection. And again, these exhortations boil down to the great commandments to love God with all of one's being, and to love our neighbor as ourselves. See Mt 22:35-40.

Finally, it must be acknowledged that under the rubric of Orthodoxy, God has, in the mystery of his will, allowed a staggering diversity of expression, failure, and mystery. We are "seeing through a glass darkly." It is good to remember that our ethos should be in the Word and grace of God. We should ponder and purpose the changes this might require, and avoid the endless proliferation of mistrust and schism, which has been one of the unfortunate hallmarks of the Protestant church. Likewise, in the formation of a Christian ethic for the modern church, an emphasis should be placed, as stated earlier, on the clearest mandates of Scripture. We will develop this thought fully in the last section. Last, we should remember that we are all imperfect human beings.

As of 2020, I am forty-six years old. I have spent most of my life in church. I consider myself, at the institutional level at least, to be "de-churched." I have attended a home church for several years. I began teaching English as a Second Language at a local Baptist church a couple of years ago, which is at the time of this writing suspended due to the Covid-19 pandemic. I meet with friends at times for spiritual encouragement, although I would like to develop my spiritual circle further. I have a few credits of graduate study with Denver Seminary and have been reading a lot on my own for about five years now as I ponder this book. I know my prayer life could use improvement. I work as a firefighter in a town of around two hundred thousand people, three hundred thousand if you include what we are now calling a metroplex. I am a Lieutenant in the fire department, and my total time in emergency services is close to sixteen years. My future in emergency services is uncertain due to the pandemic and the physical and psychological toll it has taken on me. Theologically, I am currently undecided on the whole Calvin/Arminius beef, although after being raised in what I would consider an abusive Arminianism, I have been drawn to the grace of God I encountered in such figures as Martin Luther, Brennan Manning, Henry Nouwen, NT Wright, and others. I lean a bit toward the reformed side now, but not all the way... I still suffer severe crises of faith and dark nights of the soul as a matter of course. I feel inadequate for the task of writing this work, and so many other things.

Born in 1974, I was raised attending an Assembly of God church. My earliest recollections are of Sunday school. Our teacher was a lady with an enormous bouffant of red hair who sat in a giant red rocking chair. We did the standard stuff of the era. Paper figures on felt boards illustrated the core biblical stories of Moses and the Israelites, the exploits of David, Mary, and Joseph, and the life of Jesus. We made crafts with construction paper, glue, crayons, and macaroni. Often, I would encounter the pastor in the foyer, who invariably would shake my hand and ask me how high I could jump. I could smell his cologne, hear the rustle of his grey suit, and feel the warmth of his handshake. We then walked down the hideous mauve carpet that remained a staple there for decades, and took our place on one of the pews, antiqued by a local carpenter and layman of the church.

I was born and raised to the age of three in Amarillo. Then my father was transferred to El Paso with his job at Levi-Strauss. We stayed there for five years. During that time, sometime between the ages of four and eight, I suffered sexual abuse at the hands of an older kid in the neighborhood. One afternoon, in my third-grade year, my sister and I were pulled out of our class at school and, without explanation, moved back to Amarillo that day, staying for a brief time with relatives during the move and house search.

My father started what seemed a miserable job at the Owens-Corning fiberglass plant. The crazy shift work exacerbated his epilepsy, and he had frequent seizures, the mere threat of which I experienced daily. It was profoundly traumatic to me. I believe the seizures contributed to severe depression on his part. This depression, together with anger at his general situation and fatigue from work, left him with a cruel temperament and bound to the couch for most of my growing up years. This caused an all-around depression and malaise around the house. It was an atmosphere where feelings were not shared, and shame and anger were prevalent.

There were other incidents of trauma for our family in the early years of our return to Amarillo. My mother lost a baby at seven months gestation, for whom we had a full-blown funeral. My sister and I were beat up by a group of Hispanic kids at the park, just because. There were a handful of bullies in that neighborhood it seemed, a few of them Hispanic. On one occasion, I found an injured bird at the park. I picked it up to take it home when two of the aforementioned intercepted me. They took the bird from me, laughing, and decided they wanted to make him "fly again." With that, they threw the bird repeatedly back and forth across the park until it died.

My mother went through another traumatic pregnancy, which initially manifested in an episode of severe bleeding for which I, at age eleven, had to call the ambulance. The indifference with which the ambulance crew treated us made an impression on me that has informed my practice for my entire career. I always try to remember the kids and family members on our scenes.

A Christian Ethic for the Modern Church

During my mother's hospital stay, we were returned for a time to the relatives we had stayed with during the move. My mother's pregnancy ended with a life-threatening hemorrhage and the premature birth of my younger brother on my twelfth birthday. The events inside and outside the home during this period precipitated a darkness that rent our family. Much of the damage has followed us to this day in the form of broken relationships and functional handicaps. I have joked that our Christmas cards might read, "A Donation Has Been Made to my Therapist on Your Behalf."

We returned to our childhood Assembly of God church when we moved back to Amarillo. We must always consider the source when reading about one person's experience, but I believe my story may illustrate certain unfortunate dynamics that I have seen within the church many times. The fleshing out of a story may provide us with foundations upon which to build a healthier body.

My church then was pretribulation, premillennial, dispensational, for everyone who knows what all that means, and the implications flowing therefrom. The preaching was often loud. Prayer was a simultaneous cacophony. There were regular altar calls. There was fear of being caught smoking or masturbating when Jesus returned and being *left behind*. The undercurrents of shame, fear, and paranoia kept us in an exhausting state of spiritual anxiety that still affects me.

As children, we were regaled with stories of Satanists murdering people just so they could "run their hands" through their victims' insides, of people who had advanced so far in Dungeons and Dragons that they had gone outside and blown their brains out when their in-game characters were killed, of lost Black Sabbath albums that demonically controlled their owners, a traveling evangelist whose tale opened at a scream and never relented, whose daughter had been violently raped at a rest stop by men who had "used a steel rod on her." This was the "Satanic Panic" of the eighties, a time when all these things, as well as the threat of Eastern religions, Liberal Democrats, homosexuals, and other bogeymen, dominated religious discourse at irrational and neurotic levels among many evangelicals. All this took place alongside the political heyday of the Religious Right.

Alcohol, sex, drugs, smoking, rock music, and profanity were the devil. Masturbation was beyond mention in its shame. The world "out there" was going to hell in a handbasket, and we knew who to blame. But, had we considered the deleterious effects of unbridled capitalism, our history of slavery, racism, and genocide, the poor in our neighborhoods, the mentally ill and ostracized languishing under our own church roof? What about unjust wars and atrocities, systemic injustice? Had we taken a hard look at paternalistic and transactional missions and ministry? Did we even understand or care how the violent stories and the fear and shame-based preaching would affect the children we had been given to steward? Had we considered the beam in our own eye? Perhaps to do so with honesty would teach us how much it hurts, and make us sensitive to the plight of *those others, out there*. What about the unity of the Body and the Agape love of Jesus toward the broader world? Had we found a way to look at the world with a salutary intent, rather than a militant and accusatory one? As an adult, I would find that, indeed, people like Francis Schaeffer, Jacques Ellul, Henry Nouwen, and many others had been sounding the alarm.

Much of the rigid and shame-based dynamic transferred readily to my home. It was horrifying for my folks to discuss sex. The talks usually lasted one sentence or less. We did not talk much. We did not eat together as a family. We did not have the latest fashions. I was socially awkward. The abuses I suffered caused no small amount of social dysfunction for me. One of the most repugnant aspects of all of this is the religiosity and *church-speak* that goes along with the abuse. I believe that spiritual abuse causes particular types of injuries that are difficult to heal, and that is one of the reasons Jesus was so harsh with the Pharisees, lawyers, and scribes. This is Jesus fighting for grace, fighting for sinners. I believe he would say the same truths to so many of us today *because he loves sinners and wants us to come to him.*

The difficulties were amplified in the church setting. As a young person, I sat under an angry God in an institution where the adults were angry Gods with skin on, and I felt the rejection of my peers as well.

In my perception, the church was no different than school or the rest of life. You were either "in" or you were "out," and I always felt "out." Even here I must allow for perception versus reality. I acknowledge that existing difficulties can make it hard for a person to receive acceptance from others, even when that is what he or she craves, and even when it is actually being offered. It becomes a vicious cycle. But, my experiences as a young person in a moralistic church, and later experiences of perceived rejection, cause me to reflect on the need for Christians to go "outside the gate [and bear] his reproach" to provide a needed community for hurting folks. See Heb 13:13. And we must remember that healing takes time and patience.

Let us digress for a moment with a quote from Balmer and Winner's work on Protestantism in America, "Institutionally, Protestantism has contributed schools, colleges, universities,

On the Institution of Church in America

orphanages, nursing homes, and hospitals to the American landscape . . ."[1] They go on to discuss Protestant contributions to art, music, architecture, philosophy, and social justice, as well as the Church's contributions to life, meaning, community, and "rubrics and ceremonies to mark the passages of life."[2] It has been noted in historical writings of the early Church era that the sanctity of life was exalted by the nascent Christian church. The abolition movements were largely born of a Christian ethic. We could go on at length about the contributions of Christianity and the Judeo-Christian ethic; indeed the West has constructed an entire worldview from this rich history. But, that history often obfuscates many blatant and egregious injustices, and it has been blended deftly with politics, patriotism, capitalism, and the war-making machine so that one touches it at his or her own peril.

It is easy to decry outright abuses to the faith, and indeed we have, but more important at this hour, I think, is the need to expose and repent of our complicity with injustice, and our compromise with the spirit of this age. It may be true that much of it has come from a willing stubbornness, but it is likely that we are socialized to the status quo, and cannot conceive of alternate psychological or practical frameworks. I contend that there are better ways of being in this world that are less harmful, less wasteful, more innocent, more meaningful, more full of healing, and more glorifying of God. There are ways of being that will allow one to reflect more positively from one's deathbed, so to speak. And, they are not far-fetched, erratic, difficult ideas. They are ideas birthed by the ethos of Jesus and the Scriptures, the nature of God, the golden rule, the saints and spiritual brothers and sisters among us, and those who have joined the great cloud of witnesses. It is up to me today to begin living up to a well-written eulogy by learning and practicing the Agape of Jesus.

Despite a painful hip injury incurred at birth, my mother became an elementary school teacher, and in her seventies is still teaching at a Montessori school. During my childhood, she often taught children with various special needs, including those who were emotionally disturbed. When she had some deaf students and wanted to learn to communicate with them, she went to sign language classes, though I was oblivious to this. The sign language teacher had also started a church for the deaf community and at one point my mother took us kids to visit. We had all been struggling in the old AG church. My father had dropped out altogether by this time anyway, so my mother figured it would help not only with her sign language skills but maybe our church situation as well. I was in my mid-to-late teens, my sister being two years my junior, and my brother three or four years old.

Through much trepidation, we visited the deaf church. It was in the heart of the San Jacinto neighborhood, a troubled area that is to many an object of scorn, and the subject of civic meetings, religious ministries, and general consternation. We pulled into the dirt parking lot of a tiny, white, pier-and-beam building that couldn't have been more than two thousand square feet. We were apprehensive. None of us kids had ever met a deaf person. We had no idea what to expect.

It was apparent upon entering the building that we were not in Kansas anymore. The first thing that no hearing person could avoid noticing was the awkward cacophony of deaf persons' near unintelligible voices. We were accosted by J, a deaf girl with severe mental disabilities. She smiled incessantly. She slobbered as much, and she signed to us, not knowing that we had no earthly idea what we had just walked into. She was a very sweet spirit through whom God could teach us volumes if we would stop to listen.

We met Jerry and Linda, a deaf couple who to this day help hearing folks learn sign language. Linda now works with my mother at the Montessori preschool. Their son Robert was my age and we became instant buddies.

We met the pastor and his wife. They were kind to us. Their son Jason would, indeed, go outside the gate and be my friend. *The warmth of these people carried us over the initial awkwardness.* In no time at all, we were learning some basic sign language. We were invited to eat with our new church friends in their homes or stay the night. Although I was still struggling socially and near the nadir of my teenage rejection and despair, I found a lifeline in a tiny deaf church in the middle of a troubled neighborhood.

As we got to know these folks, they inquired about my father, and secured permission for a couple of the men to come and visit him. These men of the church came to my home and through loving admonition, convinced my father to rise from his sickbed and walk. He began attending the deaf church and has been in church ever since.

I was nearing the end of high school and my prospects for a future felt dim. I was, I believe, mentally ill by this time, and neither understood nor was availed of any treatment. I hated school and did not have the ambition or the funds to attend college. I was drinking too much. I had a job bagging groceries at a local supermarket and a few work buddies with whom I would spend the last couple high school summers drinking and hanging out.

During one of my shifts at the grocery store, a Navy recruiter visited me. I would have been averse to considering the military up to that time, but I was struck at that instant with the idea of a way out of the hopeless grey I felt in Amarillo. My time in the Navy started in an exemplary fashion and ended in failure. I will touch on that story in a moment.

Shortly before I departed for the Navy, the deaf church faced an issue familiar to many churches. We were outgrowing our tiny building. We found a larger, two-story place about a mile away on a more prominent corner. I suppose it had been another church before that. The parishioners were excited about the move, and several of them co-signed for a loan on the new property. I got to spend a little time in this building before leaving for the service. My experience with the deaf church was an oasis in the desert.

I left for boot camp on October 22, 1992. With one exception, I would not darken the doors of a church again until August of 1997. I suppose in this sense I am not much different from many young people. I will not count the farcical "church" meetings in boot camp, which were little more than indoctrination. Every meeting ended with the video of Lee Greenwood's "God Bless the USA," which, in the context, really wasn't about God, it was about imprinting the narrative of religious nationalism, blatantly conflating faith and patriotism.

After basic training, I went to a Navy "A" school. In my case, it was the Interior Communications Electrician (IC) course. We learned how to work on alarms, communication equipment, navigation equipment, and anything that made a noise or a signal. The class was held in San Diego.

There was a man who came every Saturday to the base and witnessed to us sailors. I have to admire his courage and persistence in the face of such little return. He invited us to church. For some reason, I agreed to go one Sunday. One of my buddies went with me. We found ourselves in a rather raucous, Pentecostal meeting, ... lots of singing, standing, shouting, dancing ... and a sermon somewhat reminiscent of my childhood. After church, we were fed a hot dog lunch out in the California sun while a breeze wafted through the overhead tarps. Even though I was raised among them, I now felt awkward among these Pentecostal, conservatively dressed folk. We made a hasty exit and did not return.

During my time in the Navy, the deaf church folded back in Amarillo. The building was sold to another church and another ... The last time I was in the area, it was still a church. There are lots of iron bars and gates on the building now, as the neighborhood has continued to struggle.

Upon my return to Amarillo, I was in every way a mess. Apart from literally eating pig slop, I was the prodigal son. I had lived in San Diego, Newport News and Norfolk, Virginia, and Brooklyn, New York. I'd been in rehab for alcohol. I had been in trouble. I had been in and out of ridiculous and heartbreaking relationships. I had been beaten up physically. I had been annihilated emotionally and spiritually. I had squandered time, money, and opportunity through foolish behavior, causing many regrets that I am still working to overcome.

During my Navy time, I had been beaten enough by alcohol that I tried my best to stay sober after they sent me to rehab. For the most part, from late 1993 onward, I stayed away from alcohol. There were, however, unfortunate periods later in life when I would do battle and lose again. I left the Navy in June of 1996, lived briefly in Brooklyn, and returned to Amarillo a wreck.

I did not readjust well. I had returned in defeat. I initially reconnected with friends and relatives, an "adult" now, and ironically brought a measure of "youth" back to the scene. I wanted to party all the time. We all went out.

I was not well. I could not hold a job. A couple of brief and disastrous relationships came and went.

Some Baptist folks came knocking at my door one day while I blasted the song ADIDAS, by the band Korn, on my stereo. The acronym stands for, "All Day I Dream About Sex." They gave me a gospel tract and a church invite.

By this time I was a "wake and bake" guy. I got up, took drugs, and passed back out. I had lost a couple of jobs. I lived, for a minute at least, in a rental property.

One morning, a strange scraping sound filled the house. Then came the din of gospel music. I crawled out of my tweed, thrift-store chair and peeked through the blinds. A thin, grey-haired white man was scraping the paint on my house. He wore a blue and white plaid shirt and wire-rimmed glasses, and a long-ashed cigarette hung from his lips. Gospel music. Damn.

The south end of the house was the size of a barn and clad in two-and-a-half-inch siding, so the scraping went on for days. It was a cruel and unusual punishment for him *and* me. The gospel music also went on for days. It was agonizing. One day, the man knocked on my door and I let him in to use the bathroom. He walked in, past a cannabis plant I had growing in my miserable abode. I had run off all my friends by this point. So, in the spirit of "can't beat 'em join 'em," I asked *Steve* if he needed help scraping paint. I was hired. Steve was an old hippie-slash-country guy turned Christian. We started doing a little work together painting and remodeling for the landlord of my rent house.

We went to Steve's house for lunch one day and I met his family. He had a wife and two teenage daughters. All four of them smoked like freight trains, and all four of them were in love with Jesus. He took me to church one day where I witnessed their exuberance in worship. Steve would later admit to me that seeing that cannabis plant was a sore temptation to him, and he had asked God if he were sure he had the right guy for the job. As a side note, I have softened my beliefs about cannabis after much research into the smear campaign America has been subject to and experiencing some of its benefits for PTSD.

During this time my mental and spiritual illnesses came to a crisis point and I drank again after several years without alcohol. During my drunk I did some damage to my rent house, cutting my hand in the process. The ambulance took me to the hospital where a doctor put stitches in my hand. My dad showed up with his pastor. They didn't talk to me much at the time because I was so drunk. Since my dad was there with a clergyman, I was released to them and not sent to the psychiatric unit.

My father took me to his and my mother's house. On the way, I blathered on about all of my griefs and problems. At my parents' house, I was given a pillow and a blanket. I slept off my drunk on the floor of their living room.

The next day I awoke to the presence of my father and the Pastor, who at the time presided over the church I had attended as a child. He opened his Bible to first Corinthians, the sixth chapter, and began to read the ninth verse, "Know ye not that the unrighteous shall not inherit the kingdom of God? Be not deceived: neither fornicators, nor idolaters, nor adulterers, nor effeminate, nor abusers of themselves with mankind, nor thieves, nor covetous, nor *drunkards,* nor revilers, nor extortioners, shall inherit the kingdom of God." It was very nearly a checklist of my sins.

He continued, "Now you can think about it, but I may not be here tomorrow to pray with you."

Of course, I had thought about it. I had been thinking about it all my life. My upbringing, with all its abuses, its silence, its shame, guilt, and fear had been thoroughly suffused with church, the Bible, and Christianity. Those were the reasons I had fled the Church in the first place. This is a sore indictment of the *zeitgeist* and the institution, and one that I want to give voice to for others.

Nevertheless, I was at the end of my rope. I had made compulsory and awkward declarations of faith as a kid, but this was a different moment. One thought plastered itself across the landscape of my mind, "If this doesn't work, I'm going to have to kill myself."

Let us pray.

I knelt down beside my parents' couch and cried out, "Jesus, I can't live this way anymore. Please save me!"

We stood up and prayed and talked some more, and as we walked the pastor to his car, I heard music playing inside me. I cannot explain it, but I will testify to it until my dying day.

That Sunday as I ascended the steps to the baptismal font of my childhood church, I felt the presence of God. I was the wretched prodigal, blackened eyes, gaunt, stitches, ugliness all plunged into the cleansing flood. Blood. Water. Spirit.

Up I came. There was one of the church men, Al Osborn, with a towel, trembling under the weight of God's presence. They had been praying for me for years, through the nightmare of my alcoholism, and my exile to a far country. They were witnessing the firsthand answer to their long and fervent prayers. This is the testimony of my salvation experience.

I wish I could say it has been roses ever since, and of course, God never promised it would be.

On the Institution of Church in America

Al Osborn took me under his wing right away. For months, he would pick me up at my parents' house where I was staying, having been evicted a week or so after the drunken incident at the rent house when the landlord happened to see the damage. Al picked me up early on Sunday mornings, and we would go into the church while it was still quiet and empty. I saw him walk around the sanctuary, praying, contemplating, worshiping, and listening for God. I began to emulate this habit, and still do.

After prayer, we went outside and Al warmed up the church buses. Al and his wife, Cindy, had drafted me into the bus ministry at once. We drove North Amarillo picking up kids for Sunday school. I remember many of them still. One gaggle of siblings lived in absolute squalor. They had no socks, and their shoes were broken, mismatched, and often on the wrong feet. They were dirty. Their mother would often see them off with an infant on her hip and one in her belly. It made me angry.

At another house, a brother and sister lived with their grandparents. They were diminutive white people as if they had been malnourished when they were very young, but Grandma always presented them well... hair combed, he in a neat little suit, and she in a pretty dress. They were like miniature adults you might see in a fairy tale movie. I wonder where they are now.

We rounded them up, with so many others, and took them to church where they were loved, preached to, jacked up on candy, and put back on the bus to go home.

After all of this, Al and his wife would have me to their home and we would eat lunch together. Al would talk to me all day about God and the Scripture. We would then doze off until Sunday evening church. This went on for no small length of time. This family loved me in their home. They grew to trust me enough to watch their house while they went out of town. Al and I went fishing. I remember these things more than anything said from the pulpit.

I started working again at the grocery store I had worked at as a kid, something I swore I would never do, and this time I was stocking shelves on the night shift.

I read the Bible voraciously. I witnessed. I preached. I handed out gospel tracts. I threw out all my rock music. Any remaining acquaintances disappeared. I told the pastor one day at the altar that I had felt a call to ministry. I tried without success to do the Berean courses and work toward an Assembly of God ordination.

But there were problems. I began having constant and horrible nightmares. I had debilitating anxiety. My time alone was filled with torment. Spiritual oppression and waves of doubt crushed me every waking moment. The mental problems I had endured since childhood haunted me. None of this was being addressed and if I were to describe in detail the various torments of that time, I think few people would believe me.

Close to two years later, with not a single date the whole time, I met the woman who would become my wife. I moved out of state to be with her, to a small town, to the chagrin of some of my church associates. One of her coworkers took us to their church, a nascent charismatic ministry that was housed in an ancient, three-story high school building.

Prophecies were rampant in this church. The pronouncements were made regularly about how God's glory was going to descend on the place, and those dusty, empty halls were going to be filled with a new kind of students from all over the world, hungry for God. It would be a launching pad for unimaginable ministry. The offering times were accompanied by chants of, "Money COMETH!" There was always a short message implying that we would be rich if we gave. Checks would arrive in the mail. Bonuses would come from nowhere at work. A little seed for a big need. It was prosperity gospel stuff. Lots of strange messages were shared from that pulpit. We finally had to leave. The pastor hung up on me when I gave him the news that we would not be returning. He later moved out of state for another ministry opportunity. Sometime later, the church folded.

However, while we were there, my wife's coworker and her fiance *had us over to eat*. I had stopped in to see Steve (another Steve!) once before while he was remodeling his bathroom. He talked about how he didn't know any real ministers that had not been through a "strippin' down" before they were sent out. We had the first of many meals with this couple, and we were soon fast friends.

Steve had perceived several years before our meeting that God was calling him to go to northern Finland and share the gospel. Why northern Finland who knows. Steve believed that a minister is worthy of his hire as the Bible says, and so he believed that his "calling" meant he should only work at the church. He spent his days mowing the church grounds, painting, doing repairs, and doing anything else they asked. I am not sure they were even paying him, and I think they were taking advantage of him, but he refused to work anywhere else. In addition, he would not go to Finland until he felt that God had given him the official green light. There seemed to be no rhyme or reason to the process, and he could be frustrating in his obstinacy about these points.

Meanwhile, there were circuit-riding "prophets" that would make the rounds of the small towns and independent churches in the area. In hindsight, it seems a bit suspect, but at the time many of us put tremendous stock in "getting a word" from God through these prophetic utterances. They tended to be either swelling orations about coming glory and blessings, acknowledgment of wounds, or predictions of events in a person's life. Although I believe wholeheartedly in the gifts of the Holy Spirit, the skeptic may rightly expose a lot of this behavior as charlatanism. I wonder sometimes where were the exhortations to holiness, the great commandments, simple kindness, practical ministry, sanctification, or the Sermon on the Mount.

The impulse to power, the potential for abuse, and the amount of confusion that can be wrought by the misuse of spiritual gifts are immense in our current spiritual and psychological framework. This cannot be overstated. Until the Western Church experiences a profound psychological reorientation, our *charismata* might be better manifested in the meeting of daily needs, our words of wisdom and knowledge as direct quotes from the Word of God, and how we can be obedient to Jesus. Our gifts of miraculous healing might be better expressed by bringing someone to the dinner table and adopting them into our community without expecting anything in return, even a confession of faith. The exercise of spiritual gifts should come from the Agape love of Jesus, from mature Christians. It should agree with the Scripture. It should be absent of manipulation and the psychology of utility, objectification, and transaction. It should not be about me *exercising a gift*. It should compel us to holiness and practical good works.

The time came and Steve went to Finland. Through many tribulations, he helped start a church just south of the arctic circle. He speaks Finnish now and he moved back some years ago for purposes of his daughter's education. It has been over twenty years since he began the endeavor. I never saw that Steve had any oversight or accountability, no community of Christian people to surround him in his work. It has been difficult for me to fully understand the mind of God in that situation. Maybe it's none of my business. Maybe it is the lot of an apostle. Steve regularly makes trips to Finland to minister. However, he now spends most of his time in the states.

We reconnected with Steve and his wife over the last couple of years. They are sweet and hospitable people. Our reunion filled me with the sensation that no time had passed at all. Our teenage daughters found an instant friend in their teenage daughter. When we get together, we laugh and we eat until we are full to bursting.

Back to Amarillo

The majority of our now twenty-one-year marriage was spent at only two churches which I will attempt to somewhat anonymize and generalize. I would like to conduct a brief survey of my experiences good, bad, and ugly, and without vitriol, highlighting several systemic phenomena that seemed to crop up regularly and which warrant attention. I wish to handle this part with a delicate touch because many of us could rant and rave about offenses, real or imagined, suffered at the hands of *the Church*.

Social and institutional difficulties tend to fall into the categories of money and power, church governance and structure, social relationships, and spiritual development. I will try to focus on the institution itself, although there may be some overlap with things we have already discussed. We will also look at the intractability of some of the internal problems of the church. For example, the current sexual issues the church is facing are multi-faceted. We must face sexuality and the Church internally, and how we will shape doctrine and praxis. We must also develop a workable interface with the wider world, that allows for love, exchange, and movement while preserving the integrity of belief. At stake in the development of doctrine is not "love" in the latest culturally defined sense, but the very *imago Dei* itself, as the true identity of the human being, contra the current "identity politics" scheme, which I believe is producing profound confusion and pain among humanity, particularly our young people who are being raised on it. Healing for humanity is in a right understanding of ourselves as revealed by God in Christ. Collapsing all of this into just one or two issues, or shooting our theology from the hip does violence to all involved, whereas a different paradigm could help the Church move past so much of the bitter and stalemated rhetoric that is damaging her witness. After this brief survey, we will examine ethical models that the Church might consider at the organizational level.

My wife and I returned to Amarillo after her workplace closed in the aforementioned small town. I had been working for an electrical contractor. I found similar work back here in Amarillo, and, oddly enough, soon found myself contracted out to that same dark satanic mill at which my father was employed. It was a surreal sensation, seeing as an adult the dreary place at which my father had spent so many years working to keep a modicum of food on the table. A few times we ate lunch together there. The place was hot and sticky, and every surface was covered in fiberglass, as I would be after every shift, as my father was for twenty-three years before moving on to other work.

Soon enough, the electrical work dried up and I was laid

off. I started attending classes at our community college and started working quite against my will at a grocery store up the street. I also worked for a while at a coffee shop.

In Amarillo, we began attending a large church. We sang in the choir for a while. We availed ourselves of pastoral counseling more than once. I experienced an interpersonal difficulty with one of these counselors when it seemed that a friendship was developing and then was abruptly abandoned. As I had gone to him initially for pastoral counseling, perhaps *he* made a mistake in crossing a professional boundary in the first place. I don't know, but I perceived it as a hurtful rejection. We had other counseling experiences that were normal and helpful. There, I received some direction and wisdom that I still think about today. I have received the benefit of healing and deliverance ministries, often fringe topics for discussion, but I believe my experiences were genuine. I had some hokey experiences too.

The "prophetic ministries" were a mainstay in this large charismatic congregation, as they had been in the small-town church. I will again assert that new psychology is needed before we seek and emphasize the more esoteric "spiritual gifts." Until then, perhaps we would be best served by sticking to "spiritual milk" and mobilizing every bit of the laity in practical ministry.

I remember once in Kansas watching a Western missionary introduce a foreign minister who had for fifty years worked in an area hostile to Christianity. In contrast to the harsh, even smug, tone of this particular Westerner, this foreign man spoke gently, and with crushing power about prayer and the love of God for humanity revealed in Jesus Christ. The weight of his spiritual grace was palpable, and the simplicity of his message was a stark and disturbing contrast to so much of the self-serving weirdness inherent in our "Christian" culture. I had the privilege of shaking his hand and the undeserved honor of being called "brother" by him. A bowl of hot soup to a hungry soul is worth a thousand of some of our so-called prophecies.

In our new church, we found a home group. Most of the people there were closer to our parents' age and of a considerably higher socioeconomic status. Most of the group members were white folks, except me; I am white and Hispanic. An African-American couple joined our group at one point. My wife and I grew up economically poorer, and in various social situations. It has been a work to find our place in the world, and for me to overcome my prejudices.

These people received us into their homes in the Sleepy Hollow neighborhood with warmth. At the time it was among the nicest subdivisions in town, although thanks to our unbridled expansion, it has been eclipsed twenty times over.

The life group leader was one of the church pastors, a bit of an outlier as far as accessibility is concerned because we were able to meet with him every week. He was a gentle soul, one who embodied Jesus' manner of whom it is said, "A bruised reed he shall not break, and smoking flax shall he not quench . . ." Human he was, as his daughter once reminded us, but nevertheless an exceptional man. He is an example of why it is excruciating to write a work like this, because he seemed such a gentle soul, about the Father's business, but working in a dehumanizing manifestation of this thing we call church. I would so often seem to paint so many with the same broad brush and in the same poor light. It is grievous, but necessary to look at the overall picture of our institution. We must look at overall impacts on society, *and* how the construct impacts individuals as well, both within and without. The surgery allegory seems to apply here. We inflict a wound with the good intention of removing infection and facilitating healing.

Our life group leader was in a serious motorcycle accident in Colorado. He did not die immediately, and so great prayers and supplications went up for him, along with prophecies of miraculous healing. Were we weak in faith? Deluded? Or, did the Refiner of silver, having removed the dross, see his reflection in his work and pull the piece from the fire?

What is remarkable about this incident is the speed with which this man's poor grieving widow seemed to be abandoned because she wasn't "getting over it" quickly enough. This reflects, I submit, not only our discomfort and disconnect from the human condition, but also our formulaic and utilitarian mindset: "You should be better by now. We've got to get on with it." I would ask, "With what?"

This is one example of a larger systemic problem. Massive organizations, be they sacred or secular, tend *inevitably* toward EFFICIENCY, manifested as depersonalization. As we discussed earlier, this is the requisite foundation of hatred, oppression, racism, inequality, and distorted manifestations of ministry. I am not accusing these people of these things in particular; I am suggesting that the psychology which is ingrained in our society drives us, even in our "spiritual" ventures, into a dehumanized and utilitarian construct that is difficult if not impossible to escape at the institutional level. Rather than take a critical look at the model itself, we have so often tried to sanctify the model through the expenditure of phenomenal amounts of energy, money, and ingenuity. We have tried to build living organisms out of machine parts.

Although our time with this particular group was meaningful, we never did engage in any real, organic community for the rest of our time at that church. Part of the reason, to be fair, is that we began having kids, so our time constraints and priorities changed.

This large church had lots of projects and ministries going on. Sundays were the aggregation of a giant crowd before the stage to attend the rock concert worship service and hear a dynamic message by a dynamic speaker. The kids had all been whisked off to various dynamic programs.

Of the Sacraments, so to speak, the Eucharist, or communion, did not have a central, or a high place there to my recollection. Baptisms were carried out during "special services" in a separate chapel, during a separate time. Regardless of one's personal beliefs about the Lord's Supper and Baptism, ought not these dynamics give us pause?

I began to feel like a number in a seat. A definite "do not cross" line between clergy and laity developed and hardened. I was angered by the constant displays of affluence, and the undercurrent of classism. I was fodder for the organization. Sundays at the building were the product, and all of us were the consumers.

In such a situation, I was forced to wonder what I would be doing to another human being by bringing them to this place, making them a part of it, because in that construct, that would be the definition of evangelism. This is a weighty question. When I invite someone to my house for dinner, or out for a cup of coffee, I am extending an offer of relationship, friendship, or fellowship. These relationships may be of various levels, but in a giant organization, no such potential contract or covenant exists. In the case of a massive, modern American church, am I simply inviting another consumer to take their place next to me in the seat? Even the home groups, which attempt the development of an organic community, often tend to support the inorganic and utilitarian nature of the institution. If you doubt, go to Disneyland, then to a mega-church on a Sunday, and compare the two experiences. You will arrive at a security-controlled, color-coded parking lot. You'll eventually enter the gates and print out bar-coded stickers for your children and drop them off at designated classrooms. Staff representatives will be stationed throughout the building to answer questions and control the flow of traffic. There are likely armed security guards on mics stationed throughout. Then you will be treated to a well-polished, scripted, and time-bound production.

If you are part of the staff or worship team, you might have some relationships, although they tend to be centered around the doings of the organization. You will have a book full of church lingo, and you could be fired at a moment's notice. We had observed an ascendant assistant pastor, whom we were fond of, step up to the podium one Sunday and flatly announce that he was too immature and was leaving. Huh?

In time it became apparent that this mega-center was not mega enough. The talk from the front turned increasingly toward money and giving. Ministers from big cities came in and talked about . . . money and giving. A building campaign was announced. Oh, what glory of God will be able to descend!

We are outgrowing our building, praise God. A financial guru on the radio counsels us to avoid debt like the plague. He says wouldn't it be better to write a ten-thousand-dollar check to your local church, than to the interest on your house payment. That check to my church is now going to an even bigger, much bigger, house payment. I would rather use those ten thousand dollars to do something that directly helps someone, and not just feeds into a corporatized machine with enormous and unnecessary expenses.

A Christian Ethic for the Modern Church

Churches like these often have satellites in other towns and a variety of outreach ministries. Doubtless, many people love it, and arguments could be made for the efficacy of many things they are doing. Nevertheless, the manipulative preaching about money, the frequent building projects, the inaccessibility of the managerial elite, the massive amount of resources a facility like that requires just to keep the lights on, and the depersonalization of the Sunday morning production combined to convince me more and more that something was broken in how we think as a people.

It is safe to assume that many of the individuals, the outreaches, and the hearts of many of the leaders of the megachurch have been portrayed unfairly by my blanket remarks, and that is regrettable. I have not sat at the table to hear the hearts of these leaders, and in many cases *could not* have done so, due to their inaccessibility! In any case, it is the institution we face, and the psychology behind it that must be dismantled. Although institutions are made up of individuals, I submit that they are more than the sum of their parts by virtue of their entrenchment in our psyche, by their *mythic* power.

And to be fair, does not each individual Christian bear the responsibility to pursue holiness and good works, to fulfill the great commandments to love God and neighbor? While this is true, it is evident in Scripture that we are not meant to do this in isolation, hence we have The Church, to which we look for the norms of belief and practice. I contend that historical, cultural, economic, and political influences have distorted Christian expression in our society *from the outset* and that it is incumbent upon a confessing church to recognize these distortions, confront them, and work to reform them.

Through many tribulations, we left for a smaller church,

where my wife had a relative. When I say smaller, I mean that there were maybe eight hundred people on the rolls instead of several thousand. By coincidence, we arrived the same Sunday as a new pastor.

There was a heavy emphasis on programming there: the annual choir tours, holiday productions, summer bashes, and annual banquets. Numerous families there were several generations deep. The ethos was that you joined the programming. I struggled to find spiritual sustenance there.

We joined a Sunday school class and started making acquaintances. A sweet couple, maybe ten years our senior, led the class for a while but decided to step down for personal (not moral) reasons. The interim teacher disturbed me with what I considered to be a rather harsh "works-righteousness" series of lessons. Among his later assertions to the youth were that depression and anxiety were sins. I sent an email to the youth pastor, and the head pastor asking them not to put my kids in any of his classes. I made myself available to discuss the matter in person. My emails were not answered. Again, I wish to be fair, these are busy people who may not have time to answer every email from a parishioner. I give them grace.

I had the opportunity to begin teaching the adult Sunday school class, and tried to fill what seemed to me, a significant spiritual need. I taught classes on what the Bible is and how we got it, expounded the basic cardinal doctrines drawn from Hebrews chapter six, and taught the (arguably slightly unorthodox) *Abba's Child*, by Brennan Manning, about the love of God.

I do not remember hearing appeals to salvation, or what I had grown up understanding as the gospel message, that we are separated from God by sin, and that we must be reconciled to God through faith in Jesus Christ, who died for us and rose again to give us life. This was confusing to me and seemed to illustrate a deep need for basic spiritual formation. They practiced confirmation for the young people, much like the Catholic church, which, I suppose, is one's confession of Christ in that tradition. I wondered about all the adults who joined the church, and many people did join the church while we were there. Part of my misunderstanding, of course, is in the fact that different traditions approach things in different ways, so please do not hear me suggest that the gospel was absent.

People, in general, there were quite cordial, although some of them could be cliquish. (We are all human!) My older daughter perceived significant social rejection there, and I observed that the young people were little different than those I had observed in the wider world. It was a familiar sensation if you will remember my recollections earlier in this work. Perhaps I was colored by my experience. There were yet many people who we really liked, and who really liked us.

Two couples moved here from Iowa. One of the guys became very involved in our Sunday school class, causing a bit of resentment by me, I'll admit. These folks were politically different than me and seemed quite outspoken about it. They infuriated me regularly, but we still became good friends. I began to consider and challenge some of the hard-line rhetoric I had grown up with, so I am grateful. This friend was also *deliberate about community*. He never ceased to get guys together, and he was good at it.

Our Sunday school class was the locus of our involvement in the church. As I said before, identity within the church was determined by involvement with its internal programming. You were a choir man, a sound guy, the youth leader, or you

On the Institution of Church in America

sat and listened. This church was involved in a number of civic and benevolent organizations as well. Sometimes we helped pack meals for kids, or did fundraisers for other groups.

As a class, we had parties to celebrate holidays and other events. The ladies had more robust prayer meetings for a while. I can remember going to prayer meetings with the two guys from Iowa, and one of the assistant pastors. For a time, I think we had within that group a measure of health and community. Many of us still have relationships on various levels. My issues and my traumatic departure from the institution caused unfortunate damage to these relationships. That is my fault. There are indeed many things I must take responsibility for, many times I should have behaved differently, fought for relationships, or been "the change I wish to see."

I remember the sickening levels of stress placed upon the staff to pull off the Christmas productions and the choir tours. But likewise, I remember some genuinely great, kind people whom I love, who felt unable to escape that stress. It was heartbreaking to watch.

I believe that many people are languishing in church pews week after week in terrible guilt, are experiencing a confusing dissonance, and are sold to an ethos of wealth to the detriment of spiritual vitality, or have given up entirely and may feel resigned to an impotent spiritual existence. Much of what might have been church activism and giving has been transferred to para-church organizations for the simple fact that people feel like their contributions are for once making a direct difference in a real person with a real need, and not just supporting a production of which they are only outside observers.

In the industrial manifestation of the church, there is no place for vulnerability or humanity. This is tragic. The ministry to alcoholics, drug addicts, and those with "hurts, habits, and hangups,"(what about sin?) is held on Monday nights at seven, among *those* people, as if the entire purpose of the gospel were not to make us understand that we are all *those* people! We have failed to recognize the common lot of humanity.

For me, it has taken an extraordinary amount of resources to begin to find significant healing and relief from my mental illness and addictions. I give all glory to God, but I must admit with sorrow that so little of this help has come through the Church. In fact, what we call the Church is, for many, salt in the wounds rather than a balm. Is it possible that God intends his body to function more like a messy and at times somewhat dysfunctional family rather than a well-oiled machine? I have read of Native American ceremonies for returning warriors. The tribe knows that the warrior has been wounded, that the horrors of war have caused his soul to be out of balance, so upon his return, he is surrounded by the village and restored to community, to balance. In other words, there are cultural mechanisms in place that allow people and societies to process and grieve change and loss. See the Father's response to the wretched prodigal! If we only understood that we are all that wounded one, that wretched prodigal, how might we be different? Even at my childhood church, I can remember my pastor, the one who asked how high I could jump as a little guy, crying out because the Church are the only ones who leave their wounded on the battlefield.

A woman in our current home church lamented that the institutional church has become focused on its survival rather than the needs of human beings. She continued by stating that Jesus is not like that. He is the one that leaves the ninety-nine to go after the one. The Pharisees dragged the "woman caught in adultery" out before Jesus and demanded that she be stoned. As Brennan Manning says, "The Pharisees would have killed the woman for the contract"[3] In our day, this is reflected in our corporate model of church administration, and in how we treat *real* sinners. So often, when the sinner arrives at the Church, at what is supposed to be *the* safe haven, he or she is rejected because the messiness of their sin would be grit in the gears of the machine, which we cannot have. If this is the case, are we not of all people the most wretched, most lonely, and most without hope? And, have we not, as a people then become the very opposite of what God intended in the revelation of Christ? It is our shame and loss when the Body of Christ this world sees is naught but a self-promoting machine.

In the midst of all this, many of the times I most felt God's presence were in the celebration of the Lord's Supper, especially when I was able to assist in the distribution of the elements. There is indeed a difference between celebrating the finished work of Christ, his presence in the Sacrament, the priesthood of believers, and the perennial Catholic insistence on intermediaries, its Protestant correlates, and, in a sense, the *un*finished work of Christ, as the priest repeats the Mass incessantly, or the Protestant laity places vicarious faith in their pastors, and even our missionaries and such, who we support with checks, and thus "satisfy" our commission to the gospel. How many of us still insist that our priests and pastors stand between us and God, whether we are aware of the fact or not? This undermines the fact that Jesus is our forerunner, who has entered into the holiest place *so that we can all follow!* See Heb 6:20. It undermines the fact that the veil was torn from top to bottom so that we could all access God on the merit of Jesus' blood. All of these things reveal to us, by God's grace, the nature and intention of God, which is *intimacy with human beings!* Why do we as leaders insist on sewing up the veil again! See Mt 23:12, Lu 11:52. The same principle continues to assert itself, ". . . he was known of them in the breaking of bread" (Luke 24:35). Further, "And they continued steadfastly in the apostles' doctrine, and fellowship, and in the breaking of bread, and in prayers" (Acts 2:42 KJV). While this may seem like a digression, I hope to show at the conclusion of the work that this is the central point.

On the Corporate Structure

We need robust theological underpinnings within the Church. We need a meta-narrative to hold us together, the common affliction of sin, and the common solution of the love of Jesus in the gospel message. We need an eschatological hope and framework of renewal. We need a fully mobilized laity, with everyone's boots on the ground in the wider world. However, the disconnect between human beings, human needs and reality, and the institution, the machine, and the program undermine these possibilities.

At a certain point in our second church, we endured another building expansion ordeal. Once again, we endured the repeated sermons on money and giving. An elaborate system of pledge cards was established, marked by weekly reminders and marches down the aisle to drop them in treasure chests, meant to emulate the Hebrew testament giving ceremony, or one of several large, clay vessels, meant to emulate the marriage feast of Cana, where Jesus turned water into money for a new building.

These funds, and the concurrent debt, would go to the addition of a new children's wing and the renovation of several older parts of the church. One parishioner pointed out that with the conversion of some of the older parts of the building to administrative offices, and despite the huge expenditure, we were netting almost zero additional space for ministry, making the project more of a remodel. I do not know if her point was considered, but the building commenced and was completed. The disconnect for me here is not that it is always wrong to build things, although, in my deepest heart, I'd like to see us as a species abandon current models of urban and suburban living, including large church buildings, for a more holistic and sustainable model. Instead, I am concerned about the psychological framework of our models. We are going to financial stewardship classes in Sunday school so we can learn to undo the generations-deep credit mentality that has enslaved us, while church leadership creates campaigns to press the laity into massive debt. I'd submit that financial stewardship programs are logically sound, but I do not see that they have addressed our fundamental bondage to mammon. We are getting out of debt to get rich, and we have seen the scriptural admonitions in 1 Tim 6:9-11, and Mt 19:24. Meanwhile, there is a whole world drowning in incalculable need. Jesus asked us to pray that workers would be sent out into his harvest, not that our buildings would be more ornate or state-of-the-art. We have neither the time nor the imperative to be rich in this world. We are told to store up our treasure in heaven. Do we believe in the truth of our promised afterlife, and God's promises of provision and renewal both here and hereafter?

To their credit, the leadership at this church put it to a vote. But who is going to say no in such a setting? In both of the building projects I have discussed, there were extensive campaigns for the project, sermon after sermon about money and giving, and pledge drives. I do not remember any rigorous discussion about alternative ideas. I voted no this time, but the project passed.

Now there is a nice new children's wing complete with classrooms, auditorium, games, toys, restaurant booths, a large welcome center, security doors, electronic check-in, and labeling. Many people find this a great place to bring their children during the week for "Mother's Day Out," or on Sundays so they can go to church.

This model appears to meet the perceived spiritual needs of many people. And, for the multigenerational families who attend, this setup is the backbone of deep-seated tradition. We can learn a lot from the structure and practice of these types of families, although the danger of insularity also exists. Further, this church supports several missionaries and allows a small African congregation to meet in the chapel on Sunday afternoons. In this, there is potential for a beneficial interface between congregations.

I believe I could interview many people who would say they love these churches, and that they felt their spiritual needs were being met. It cannot be doubted that a great number of their outreaches have been of benefit to many people, yet I will maintain that anything a large organization can do, a lot of smaller communities can do better working in concert because of the personal relationships that tend to develop in them. There may also be a growing sense among people that there must be more to spiritual life than the standard Sunday program. Many organizations have attempted to ameliorate these feelings through innovation, programming, facilities, and technology, rather than the development of a deeper internal spiritual locus and intimate community. I must empathize with

On the Institution of Church in America

sincere pastors as well whom I have heard lamenting the difficulty of appealing to our deeper hearts amid our cultural milieu.

Church governance has always been a difficult and hotly debated topic. Most of us are familiar with some of the major events that led up to the Protestant reformation. In our day we have seen the rise and disastrous falls of several high-profile ministers, followed always by an embarrassing damage control circus.

These events are easy cannon fodder for those hostile to the institution of the Church. They also wound people and drive them away. They leave us confused. We have been taught to trust in and depend on a "managerial elite" and an institutional structure, so when it fails, it is like the rug has been pulled out from under us. Consider a ministry that has great outstanding debts, such as for a new building like we discussed earlier. The moral failure of one of its leaders means the potential loss of millions of dollars and membership. It means embarrassment. It means defaulting on loans. It means the loss of livelihood for staff. It means the loss of power, influence, and money for the leaders of the organization. The potential for what is supposed to be holy to turn ugly is real.

Many would consider that, at least in the Protestant church, a spiritually robust hierarchy with organizational accountability provides at least some safeguard against the celebrity culture and/or lone-ranger independent churches in which such failures seem to proliferate. I agree with this logic in its essence, but I would argue that we do not have the cultural humility to implement these hierarchies appropriately. That is why the independents left in the first place, and so we seem to be left in a sort of catch-22.

We have spent generations treating symptoms because

A Christian Ethic for the Modern Church

we have been taught that the current structure of the church *is* the Church. We have thus made it off limits and beyond question. But, again, God has allowed a staggering variety of church expressions under the rubric of Orthodoxy. (Of course, distinguishing between what God has planned for his Church and what human beings have *done* can be tough ground theologically and philosophically.) In America, we have constructed a dizzying array of synods, conventions, dioceses, bishopricks, action committees, organizations, governments, parachurch ministries, 501.3c's, and politico-religious organizations.

The first church I talked about in this section started as a home group comprised of a handful of couples. In time, they outgrew the home setting and through prayer and deliberation decided to purchase a small church building. In time again, they outgrew their building and obtained a plot of land. They established an eldership and began to oversee satellite churches in the region.

They had several buildings on the property when we attended, and continued to build and rebuild. They launched a large ministry in another city. Their current structure is the size of a convention center. Is this how God would have it? Would I be outright dismissed for even posing the question? Francis Chan was once pastor of a mega-church, a man with much experience in practical ministry and the internal workings of the institutional church. Apparently, he walked away from it all, so there is hope. I would encourage the reading of his book, *Letters to the Church*.

One report said that, of mega-churches surveyed, "... 49% of the total budget... was spent on staffing costs, [that] 98% of a church's total budget [comes] from congregational giving... 52% of churches spent ten percent or more of their budgets on outside ministries, from soup kitchens, to world missions, to church planting."[4] This means that of the theoretical ten thousand dollar check we talked about earlier, *half* of it will go to paying the staff, a bunch of it will go to utilities, supplies, and mortgages, and only about a thousand will reach out beyond the walls of the church. And those church plants are going to be structured the same way. This is, of course, inadequate data for a full discussion on church finance, but it should give us some food for thought.

Human institutions have to interface with money, property, and authority. Could we consider a paradigm shift to funnel our money and resources more effectively toward the meeting of human needs, justice, ecological responsibility, and the alleviation of suffering? All while allowing the laity to be engaged in genuine, organic, and not contrived ministry, intimacy, and relationship with fellow believers and the wider world, not with paternalism, but as a mode of life?

It is possible. It is doable, but we must challenge the utilitarian and corporate model of church organization and governance. We will look at potential solutions in the last few sections.

7
A PROPOSED ORGANIZATIONAL ETHIC DRAWN FROM SEVERAL SOURCES

It would be easy to dismiss many of these assertions on the supposed grounds of Scripture and long tradition, but how has our overall psychology been affected by centuries of unbridled industrialization, consumption, and social engineering? When we look again at the less savory aspects of our history: genocide, slavery, environmental exploitation, the complicity of the Church with racism, and the convoluted subject of Christianity and military intervention. When we consider our many cultural and societal problems and their severity: the ever-widening wealth gap, the export of manufacturing, our loss of social structure, our crisis of meaning, our mental health and substance abuse crises, our manner of consumption, and the disdain with which we are often viewed by the wider world, we may conclude that a change in psychology and organization is worth considering. These lists could be extended, and many have laid the blame for our social and economic problems at the feet of Protestants. I believe there are many unfair distortions in this accusation, however, what we are trying to do is examine how harmful psychologies have invaded the Church in the West, understand them, and then recover models of Christian life that will bring healing to human beings, and a more Christlike engagement with the wider world.

Consider one common current church model. There is a Senior Pastor, often with Dr. in front of his or her name. There may be an associate Pastor or several, depending on the size of the church, an office staff, a corporate board, elders and deacons, worship teams, committees, and programs. Often, the individuals in the pews are not a significant part of the organization, and their "ministerial" efforts are often funneled into the dictates of what we have already termed the "managerial elite," a term borrowed from McCarraher. And, as in the industrial setting, the worker keeps his hands off the controls. He is not supposed to know how the machines work. This is textbook industrialism. So often this is the framework within which godly, loving ministers work, who really do have their parishioners' best interests at heart, whose heart's cry is to be a *shepherd*. In our modern mindset, we simply cannot conceive of alternative models, despite our persistent efforts to develop an organic community within the inorganic model, another feature of corporate manipulation. How many companies use the parlance of "family," or "team?" Do we consider ourselves or that workplace a *family*, or have we unwittingly adopted the psychology of subjugation? Many, many people are familiar with the disillusionment one experiences when they find out "what goes on behind

A Proposed Organizational Ethic Drawn from Several Sources

the scenes" at church. Many others have felt the sting when they've dared bare their humanity or their sin to a machine that has no time for grit in the gears.

We need to consider whether some of our massive denominational doctrinal expositions, and the divisions they often represent are manifestations of the love and truth of Christ, or if a greater push toward unity *a la* John 17, Psalm 133, and Acts 2 is in order.

Let us consider several Scriptures:

> "For as in one body we have many members, and the members do not all have the same function . . ." (Rom 12:4).

All of 1 Corinthians 12.

See verse 28, "And God has appointed in the church first apostles, second prophets, third teachers, then miracles, then gifts of healing, helping, administrating, and various kinds of tongues." (These are ordered most likely chronologically by need, rather than by any ranking of prestige.)

> "And he gave the apostles, the prophets, the evangelists, the shepherds and teachers, to equip the saints for the work of ministry, for building up the body of Christ . . ." (Eph 4:11-12).

> "But all things should be done decently and in order" (1 Cor 14:40).

And again, 1 Peter 5:2-3, ". . . shepherd the flock of God that is among you, exercising oversight, not under compulsion, but willingly, as God would have you; not for shameful gain, but eagerly; *not domineering over those in your charge,* but being examples to the flock." [emphasis mine] Henri Nouwen suggests that the minister of the future will be among the people, and not so much behind a pulpit, an exhilarating and terrifying thought! The above are some well-known passages on ministry that demonstrate God's intention to have function, order, and structure within his body. I encourage all of us to meditate on the tone of the passage in first Peter. Verse five of the same chapter goes on to tell us all to be clothed in humility.

Willingness. Eagerness. Submission. Examples. This is the heart from which our Christian ministry should proceed.

Our passage above from Ephesians 4 gives us somewhat of the purpose of all of this, to equip us to go out and reproduce! To build up the body of Christ. The question we must always ask ourselves is, "What are we reproducing?" Romans 8:29, KJV, states, "For whom he did foreknow he also did predestinate to be conformed to the image of his Son, that he [the Son] might be the first born among many brethren." Titus 2:14 states that Jesus, ". . . gave himself for us to redeem us from all lawlessness and to purify for himself a people for his own possession who are zealous for good works." Romans 8:18-39 develops even further the intention of God by including the created order in his plan of redemption, which brings us around to one of the main assertions of this work: God's purpose is holistic, total, corporate, and eternal. It is about our sanctification. It is about the judgment of wickedness and the consummation of all that God has made into his eternal purpose, and the restoration of his redeemed people to our original commission as co-regents with God, bearing his image eternally and without sin. All ministries should be informed by these realities.

Galatians 5:14 states, "For the whole law is fulfilled in

A Proposed Organizational Ethic Drawn from Several Sources

one word: 'You shall love your neighbor as yourself.'" Paul prefaces first Corinthians 13, the well-known chapter on the Agape love of God with this statement, "And I will show you a still more excellent way." So we see that God is no anarchist, he does command decency and good order. But, it is intended to function out of the Agape love of God in a spirit of humility.

So that we would not seem too critical or harsh, we must affirm two things. First, we are all human. We are imperfect, and our earthly endeavors will consistently affirm that, so we must always have grace and mercy for each other. Second, where God's people gather to seek him, he will be present, even amid our imperfections. He will never leave us nor forsake us. He will not leave himself without a witness. I have heard the testimony of how God has made himself known even in a state-run church in a hostile communist nation. This is an important point to consider as we critique our situation. It is easy to be of a wrong spirit or to presume upon God. That has made the writing of this work grievous. I am a clay vessel! How should I presume to critique anything, knowing my imperfection, and my sins? Surely, we must all concede ignorance when facing the endless complexities of history, government, economics, race, and everything else I have mentioned!

Even though God has promised to be present with us, and that he commands decency and good order, we are left with a mysterious dichotomy. Matthew 13:58 states, "And he did not do many mighty works there, because of their unbelief." Luke 18:8 says further, "Nevertheless, when the Son of Man comes, will he find faith on earth?" This is a question asked by an omniscient God. We are told to work out our salvation, according to the inward workings of God. See Phil 2:12. And

A Christian Ethic for the Modern Church

Jesus, as we have discussed, puts forward the admonitions to the Church *to change* in Revelation 2 and 3. So, while we are bound up corporately and individually by God's sovereign grace, there exists the potential for degradation, for the loss of faith, power, influence, and Agape. There is the ever-present danger of complicity and compromise with the spirit of this age, and the certain threat of those "wolves" setting up camp in the Church. Ellul warns of the dangers of compromise, "Church subjected by compromise with the State under Constantine. Church broken by compromise with the capitalism of the 19th century. Church deprived of revealed truth by compromise with science."[1] The command goes out to constantly endure and overcome. We meet this dichotomy by sounding the clarion call to repentance and prayer in accordance with 2 Chronicles 7:14.

These spiritual conundrums have caused me no small amount of consternation. Why has God allowed the Western Church to come to such a state? Are things really "not that bad?" In light of our historical misdeeds, our social realities, and the effects of our affluence, are we yet a "good" people? Is American affluence evidence of the favor of God? Is it really a house of cards about to fall down? Does God do part and I do part? God is indeed working in us to "will and do of his good pleasure" (Phil 2:13, cf 2 Chron 30:12). Are we not trying hard enough? Are we satisfied with the status quo to our own hurt? Should we adjust our psychological expectations and believe that everything is *exactly* as it should be because God is sovereign? Why, then, does he admonish us at all? I think the notion of the "confessing Church" *a la* Bonhoeffer is closer to the truth of our current situation, that those who can and will see things as they are, have a responsibility to embody the changes called forth in the Scripture and to bring others

A Proposed Organizational Ethic Drawn from Several Sources

along. Of the finer points of sovereignty and free will, I must plead ignorance.

Colossians 2:8,19 counsels, "See to it that no one takes you captive by philosophy and empty deceit, according to human tradition, according to the elemental spirits of the world, and not according to Christ... and not holding fast to the Head, from whom the whole body, nourished and knit together through its joints and ligaments, grows a growth that is from God." "Holding the Head" means that the primary work of the Church is relentless prayer. In this I mean all that may be called intimacy and communion with God: prayer, worship, Eucharist, gratitude, repentance, supplication, and intercession in all their varied manifestations. It is in this place that the mysterious co-laboring with God occurs. If there is no vital life of prayer and instead our energies are directed toward those things which are seen, our buildings, programs, and such, then we can become a body "functioning" without its head. Anyone who had seen an animal (or a human, I can testify) that has been dead for quite a while can tell you that a tremendous amount of activity is taking place. That activity smells terrible. Prayer changes the internal. Prayer then changes the external. Prayer empowers. Prayer softens. It is the outworking of our professed faith in the objective reality of our God. See Heb 11, Luke 18:8, James 2:14-26, 5:13-18. Prayer humbles us because we learn how weak, and how not in control we are. Programs may give us an illusory sense of control, accomplishment, or meaning, but it is just that, an illusion. Ellul continues, "Stop thinking of our action in purely mechanical terms. The Scriptures reference corn that grows, leaven that works..."[2] The real *dunamis* takes place within the mysterious communion of God and his people, where we access the living waters and receive spiritual sustenance. It is in communion with God that we most approach that for which we were apprehended by God and that to which we proceed! *Only* when this is rightly ordered, can the rest of our lives, thoughts, and actions begin to fall into place. The essence of this is the fulfillment of the first Great Commandment. And then we must get comfortable with our human uncertainty, our watering and waiting, the silence, the setbacks until *God* gives the increase. See 1 Cor 3:6. God admonishes us to patient continuance in well-doing. See Rom 2:7.

From the rightly ordered relationship to God, we have just discussed proceeds the solid ground for social ethics, activism, programs, ministries, and the like. It is the reality and nature of God that confers value upon humanity and the created order. God gives the human being her value and uniqueness, her unity, her indissolubility, her eternality. All else must collapse humanity and the creation into a meaningless and tragic nihilism despite the many complex philosophic structures that have been erected to the contrary. What else can we ultimately derive from worldviews which state that all things originated from an impersonal explosion, that there is no personal deity? Despite any protestations to the contrary, there is then no moral imperative, no grounds for a moral system, no source of ultimate meaning, and no rational or legitimate way to define or articulate good, evil, or otherwise. The enemies of Christ would talk about REASON! Let us eat, drink, and be miserable, for tomorrow we die! Beware, lest any spoil you through philosophy or vain deceit.

1 Peter 5:1-5 gives us the appropriate attitude for Christian leadership. We would do well to take a fresh, sober look at this passage. Let us also not read the word "elders" here through our modern lenses, thinking of them as those old

A Proposed Organizational Ethic Drawn from Several Sources

guys who are not the senior or associate pastors, those we sometimes call deacons. This is a crucial distortion we need to correct. We are talking about those Christians referred to in Hebrews chapter 5 who are "of full age, even those who by reason of use have their senses exercised to discern both good and evil" (Heb 5:14, KJV). We are talking about those who are clothed in humility, full of the fruit of the Spirit, and who bear the spirit outlined in James 3:13-17, pure, peaceable, gentle, easy to be entreated, full of mercy, and good fruits, without partiality, and without hypocrisy. If our pastors, deacons, and elders are not approachable, and do not display these qualities, then perhaps they are overburdened, or we need to re-evaluate our selection process. Better yet, perhaps we need to establish models of life and community that will allow for and produce such men and women. As parishioners, we may work for reform and refuse to support destructive models.

Returning to 1 Peter 5, we see that the apostle addresses the elders in the plural. The first consideration for a corporate, or organizational ethic is a significant decentralization of leadership. We can deconstruct our pyramid, and consider the admonitions in Romans 12:4f, and 1 Corinthians 12:12-31. 1 Corinthians 12:24b-26 states, "But God has so composed the body, giving greater honor to the part that lacked it, that there may be no division in the body, but that the members may have the same care for one another. If one member suffers, all suffer together; if one member is honored, all rejoice together." The referenced Scriptures paint a picture of a body of individuals who are equal in God's sight. We are different, and we have various gifts, but God has left no place for classism. In fact, God has ". . . chosen the foolish things of this world to confound the wise" (1 Cor 1:27). If we are honest, can we not see that we esteem some too much, and some we may even ignore or disdain?

I would encourage anyone and everyone to read the book, "Twelve Steps and Twelve Traditions," written by a co-founder of the recovery program Alcoholics Anonymous. In addition to the "Steps," (Most of us have at least heard of these steps, a specific set of actions by which an alcoholic might overcome his compulsion to drink and find "a God of [his or her] understanding.") they developed a set of twelve "Traditions" which apply to the functioning of their "Society" at a group level. Page 131 states, "On anvils of experience, the structure of our Society was hammered out." Their fortunate misfortune was that they had the gift of desperation. If they did not learn to get along at the corporate level, they would not survive as individuals either. They knew this from the repeated failure of the Church, medicine, and society to make a serious impact in the treatment of alcoholism. Our problem is that we are not aware of our own desperation! The world yet goes about building the tower of Babel. We, however, must preach the enslavement of the human being to sin as the truth of the human condition, and our utter need for God. This need is real from the moment of our conception to the day we die. Our Christianity, our status before God as "saved" does not diminish this need, although we may grow in a very real freedom. Deuteronomy 20:30 tells us that God *is* our life. Acts 17:28 states, "... In him we live and move and have our being..." The good news, and the stumbling stone, is of course that God in Christ has provided salvation to humanity, *apart from our initiation.* Here is the offense and the repugnance of Babel as well; our attempts to win God's favor and mollify his just judgment by our religious observance are all in vain. 1 Corinthians 1:23, KJV states, "But

A Proposed Organizational Ethic Drawn from Several Sources

we preach Christ crucified, unto the Jews a stumbling block, and unto the Greeks foolishness . . ."

The Alcoholics Anonymous second tradition states, "For our group purpose, there is but one ultimate authority—a loving God as He may express Himself in our group conscience. Our leaders are but trusted servants; they do not govern."[3] Page 191 goes on, "All such representatives are to be guided in the spirit of service, for true leaders . . . are but trusted and experienced servants of the whole." Juxtapose these thoughts with our passages from 1 Peter 5. Then compare them with some of our current institutional models.

Further, on the point of the "group conscience," let us not think of this, for our purposes, in a *new age* sense. Let us think of Psalm 133:1, KJV, "Behold, how good and how pleasant it is for brethren to dwell together in unity." Dwell together. Impossible to achieve in a massive setting, but in the right setting and spirit, it is organic, empowering, and spiritual. Praying people, all gathered, all given a voice. Decisions are made only by substantial consensus. We might be surprised at what God reveals to us.

A decentralized leadership means no more lonely ministers, crushed beneath a burden of responsibility. It means they are insulated from celebrity, from spectacular moral failures that threaten to undo a massive organization. They, along with the group itself, are somewhat protected from the impulse to that "filthy lucre," or greed for gain mentioned in 1 Peter. It means the alienating separation between the clergy and the laity is done away with. I can access my pastors; my pastors can eat with me. It means we begin to dissolve the latent classist paradigm in the church so that all are welcome at the King's table, so that we may all be truly clothed in humility. *It was Jesus who washed his disciples' feet before his own crucifixion,* leaving us an example to follow. God help us with our mansions and private jets! We can start thinking of Church as a *group* of Christians gathered together for mutual edification, prayer, and the sharing of life, as opposed to a meeting of disparate individuals attending an event produced by a different group of people with whom we have no relationship.

Since these things are so difficult *en masse,* it leads to our second consideration, a significant downsizing of our church bodies. What about a small, intimate church that belongs *to* and *in* the neighborhood where it is located? Why not? If we are doing well, outgrowing our church, let us be missional and prayerful. Let us send out some of our people to reach another neighborhood. Local. Organic. Intimate. Our home church model has borne out the reality of the things I have asserted, in my estimation. It is certainly not the only way to do things, but I like it. It is also worth noting that when neighborhoods deteriorate, and new developments spring up, the churches tend to follow the developments, and we end up with less representation in tougher areas.

Third, we consider corporate poverty and a refusal of debt. I will define corporate poverty as the refusal of the church to amass large amounts of land, capital, or money. Ideally, the organization itself would own nothing. It is not as far-fetched as it may sound to some. The twelve-step groups have done it for a long time. The refusal of debt is just that; it is corporately obeying the Scripture which states, "Owe no one anything, except to love each other, for the one who loves another has fulfilled the law" (Rom 13:8). Even the most massive church facility in my city could only serve a few thousand of our three hundred thousand area citizens. And these large buildings, by their very existence, are huge creators of waste and consumers of resources. They often use large amounts of community infrastructure without returning anything to the tax base. There is simply no rational justification for these structures. Corporate poverty and the refusal of debts mean a lot less ugly fighting about money. Debt changes the message. It can do no other. I have to wonder how we are all doing during this pandemic. To refuse debt corporately is to display a true responsibility to those under our care.

Decentralized leadership, a downsizing of church bodies, and corporate poverty insulate us from the will to power. They make the atmosphere amenable to humility, and organic community. I know that as humans we will always have our petty squabbles, but in smaller, more intimate settings where some of these perennial snares have been removed, we have an opportunity to grow together and work these things out in love.

If we want a building, why not save up and pay cash? Better yet, let us meet in homes or lease. Did not Paul admonish us that we brought nothing into the world, and we can certainly take nothing out? See 1 Tim 6:7. The legal aspects of some of these things, because we *do* have to interface with money, can be done with minimal damage. In the step model, a group within the group may set up corporately to sign leases and such. We save up the money first. Pay out leases six months at a time, ahead of time. If something happens and God forbid the church were to fold, there would be almost zero financial aftermath. Some areas may have spaces not being used on weekends that they may be willing to allow churches to use at no or low cost. Good corporate stewardship of money allows us to do more effective outreach, insulates us from a number of serious problems, and keeps us from exploiting people with a distorted message. We can be honest and open about what is needed and how it is being used. *Many* people hold grudges against the Church because of money. A spirit of humility and corporate poverty would do much to change this.

A certain church downtown is an interesting example. They meet in an old building, and they are single of purpose. They feed hungry kids in the poorest neighborhoods in town, often making their rounds on bicycles. From this meeting of basic needs and regular visibility in the community proceed abundant opportunities to share the gospel message, alleviate human suffering, draw kids and families to Christ, and mobilize a very high percentage of the laity for direct ministry. There are very few folks there who feel "stuck" in a pew. I do not know what their leadership or financial models are like, but they seem to be making an admirable difference in the community.

Our fourth consideration concerns ecological consciousness and the care of the created order. The profound depth of this issue as it connects to not only the sharing of the gospel but also to our sanctification cannot be overstated. There is not space to fully develop this thought here, much to my regret. Please see the recommended reading list at the end of the work. I hope that all of God's people will look at the relationship of ecological care to the Gospel with fresh eyes. Here, we will look at a few points and then hopefully construct a rationale for our ethical considerations.

Laura Walls, in *Henry David Thoreau: A Life,* her excellent biographical work, points out "Thoreau's conviction that attention to the natural environment confronted the root of all political evil."[4] By extension, I would add economic

A Proposed Organizational Ethic Drawn from Several Sources

and moral evil, for it is the creation (which was made by and belongs to God) which suffers at the hands of the covetous and utilitarian. Human beings have devastated this continent. Derrick Jensen's words bear repeating, "They came also to enslave the land, to yoke it to their own purpose, and ultimately to remove from it everything of monetary value."[5] I was horrified in reading the graphic accounts of the settlement of this nation, the murders of women, children, nursing infants, the slaughter of buffalo into extinction for the sole purpose of eradicating the Indian's food supply. This happened right here where I live. All of this for industry. The list of horrors does not end. This is the mind devoid of God, devoid of love, devoid of a Sabbath, that destroys ecosystems, forests, lakes, and rivers, that drives species into extinction, that dumps poisons into the ground, the water, and the air. All of this is done to make the things we keep buying. I have gone into the grocery store and the "convenience" store, those disease dispensaries, with a more discerning eye. Plastic, plastic, and more plastic. And this is repeated the world over. This ethos, which encompasses environmental devastation on a mass scale, and human exploitation to match, was born originally in sin but came into its own with the Industrial Revolution.

James Kunstler states, "It's as if they can't imagine a world without a continuing expansion of human activities, as represented in economic growth. That is their only context."[6] As Christian people, we need to expand our context to include the created order, community development, and other human beings. We need to expand our own selves!

The exploitation of human beings and the destruction of the environment are antithetical to the Gospel, to the nature of God, to human flourishing, but they are the *modus operandi* of our industrialized reality. Jensen states further, "The US has 5% of the world's population, and consumes the majority of the world's resources."[7] The Church must change adamantly in opposition to this. To waste, to exploit is satanic. We must be rid of it. In our preaching and our practice, we must change. Warfare, genocide, human exploitation and degradation, species extinction, and loss of habitat are *all* bound up in this rapacious spirit of mammon, and the sweetest of us are implicated in it by our everyday choices. Spiritually, as we have traded the enjoined Sabbath for covetousness, we have forfeited the beauty of the created order. The Church cannot be part of the same machine that produces such devastation! So many outside the church understand this. Where is *our* witness? The blame for all of these destructions has been laid by many at the feet of evangelical Protestants! It is a great tragedy when Christians do not care for the beautiful world their Lord has made for them. See John 1:3.

Again, we must understand that this utilitarian mindset is what leads to the devaluation of the created *thing* and this extends ultimately to human beings. It is, for example, the reason that sports are multi-billion-dollar industries attended to by millions, but we can find few people who will face the daily realities of trafficked human beings (another money-making industry). To have the acknowledgment, the effort, the enthusiasm, the money, the manpower, the press coverage, and the resources, of just one pro football season exerted by the same populace against the issue of human trafficking in the United States, what damage could be inflicted on such an evil industry! The Church must preach the goodness of God's creation, austerity in the use of resources, and simplicity as a mode of life. We can construct

A Proposed Organizational Ethic Drawn from Several Sources

a recovery from the emptiness of the consumerist life, the one we have been inundated with for generations. We preach an end to buying products made in overseas sweatshops and countries with plain records of human rights abuses. Those purchases are *active* participation in human exploitation by those of us calling ourselves Christians; it is the true essence of "taking the Lord's name in vain." We hold up as spiritual heroes certain stores that close on Sundays, but where are most of their products made? Can we be agents of positive reform for those stores by demanding more local and sustainably-made products? Have we confronted the spirit within ourselves that compels the endless consumption of their goods? I believe the Body of Christ in sufficient numbers can be a force for human and economic good in this world and nation by the adoption of a holistic, humane ethic of consumption.

In doing all of this, we must recover the ethos of beauty from the Puritan ethic of work and shame, at least as the accusation goes. Dorothy Sayers believed that human beings most reflect the *imago Dei* by our creativity. It is no wonder that the industrial age brought about the division of labor whereby the thoughtful creative capacity in mankind, once wedded to his physical capacity to create the thing imagined, was cruelly removed, leaving us to produce someone else's utility with maximum efficiency. And then, a whole psychology, myth, social construct, and industry of distraction was painstakingly devised to make us believe we are happy with our lot! We work away the bulk of our healthy and active lives so that we can *purchase*. That is how they want it. Big houses. Nice cars.

Technology. Stuff. Then they give us the entertainment *industry*, to keep us docile, to keep us from acting on the underlying disconnect that tells us there must be more to life than this. It is no wonder we have such epidemic rates of suicide, mental illness, addiction, and crime. We are the most affluent society in the world. Shouldn't we be the happiest?

The reclamations of nature, beauty, art, simplicity, and contentment, are the things that damage the will of the devil and evil men. These are the things that restore dignity to humans, animals, and the creation, of which we are stewards before God. Reintegration and cooperation with the created order and others provide for health across every conceivable domain. *This is the fertile soil in which the gospel may be planted.* That is the essential idea of all we have discussed, and the reason that how we live, and how we treat the created order, matter in the sight of God. Blessed are the peacemakers. When we bring this ethos to our neighbor, to the wider world, we are then truly being Christ's ambassadors. We can then offer restoration, reconciliation, true meaning, and hope.

Fifth, the Church must make peace internally. The sexual issues are not going away. There is no use spitting vitriol at each other, and we must heed the Scripture, "For we must all appear before the judgment seat of Christ; that everyone may receive the things done in his body, according to that he hath done, whether it be good or bad. Knowing therefore the terror of the Lord . . ." (2 Cor 5:10-11, KJV.) And, "Who are you who judges another man's servant? To his own master he stands or falls" (Rom 14:4, KJV.)

Let us defend the faith. Let us dialogue. Let us make our cases. Let us agree to disagree, but let us do it with civility and respect. Does not God enjoin us even in the treatment of our enemies to bless and not curse? To pray for them? Let us not forget the faithfulness and the sovereignty of God,

A Proposed Organizational Ethic Drawn from Several Sources

"Nevertheless, the foundation of God stands sure, having this seal, the Lord knows them that are his. And, let everyone that names the name of Christ depart from iniquity" (2 Tim 2:19). Further, ". . . let him that thinks he stands take heed lest he fall" (1 Cor 10:12). This is spoken to those on *all* sides of these issues.

The truth of the matter is that Jesus said he came to bring a sword (Mt 10:34-36). The Scripture also says that judgment begins at the house of God (1 Pet 4:17). We must trust in the faithfulness of God and his sword while pursuing holiness and the fruit of the Spirit. There are no easy answers to the cultural issues of our day. As a Church, and as individuals, we are charged to live in truth. See John 17. This means that we do not have to assent to the psychologies or moral frameworks of those with whom we disagree. It also puts forward a desperate imperative for study and theological reflection. Things will become increasingly difficult for many Christians as time goes on, but we can press on in love and truth.

This internal peacemaking must then extend outside the walls of the church. Let us end the bitter political rhetoric, the bumper sticker wars, and the attempts to control our government from within. Don't watch your religious leaders trying to assert the kingdom of God through political campaigning. In our churches, let us avoid the hateful rhetoric against people outside the walls. Let us pay attention to ourselves, "eager to maintain the unity of the Spirit in the bond of peace" (Eph 4:3). This does not mean we have to compromise our internal convictions, by no means! But, let us be careful of the spirit in which we do so.

Who was the neighbor? The one who had mercy! Everywhere a Christian goes, he or she is the ambassador for

A Christian Ethic for the Modern Church

Jesus Christ. We must bear within us the mystery of God, the gospel of salvation, the antidote to the emptiness of this world. To be sure, there is beauty in this world, and among humanity. There are people of all stripes doing good. One author suggested that we should jump in any time something good is being done. Who knows, we may in that situation be able to share the truth of the human condition and the light of Christ, those precious elements that God has entrusted to us.

As ministers, we have a responsibility to speak the truth. We are to raise, "[a]wareness through the destruction of myths: social, political, media, national... [to develop and propagate a] ... will to find objective reality. To discover the facts of the people around me [and then] grasp this reality on the human level."[8] The destruction of myths means facing our past as the Church.

It means facing our present *as it is*. God's people are meant to be different from the world around us, but for many of us, that meant we eschewed fun and pleasure in all their forms, leaving us a legacy of shame and dysfunction. The further issues are deeper still, where Satan's seat is, where spiritual Babylon is. It is the confluence of political power and economic gain, complicity with the spirit of this age, and the human ignorance of our true condition.

In one example, the Church as an institution has overlooked the clear prohibitions of Jesus against divorce. Instead, we have chosen, in defiance of the hard-won (by the Baptists. Look it up!) separation of church and state, to use the issue of abortion as a political tool of power. We have used political clout and our bullhorns to excoriate all sorts of things and people *out there*. We might consider progress in making abortion unconscionable through the restoration of

A Proposed Organizational Ethic Drawn from Several Sources

the nuclear family, natural affection, and organic community, rather than illegal through our sometimes-hateful political rhetoric. One local crisis pregnancy center does just that by educating and assisting women who are pregnant, by offering them hope and alternatives to abortion, by the offer of relationships and the gospel, and by meeting basic needs, in a non-judgmental atmosphere, even if she decides to go ahead with an abortion.

They also offer parenting classes, post-abortion counseling, and all manner of youth care and education. They are now housed in what used to be the local Planned Parenthood building.

Worldwide, education programs for women seem to have prevented millions of abortions. In contrast, the draconian prohibitions on birth control asserted by the Roman church, and the political machinations of the "Religious Right" have caused untold harm. They have not drawn people to Christ, and they have not saved any babies. This is one place where the Christian religion *is* oppressive to women. We men are obligated to seek understanding of the realities of women here and abroad, and the effects of our behavior toward them. From a holistic and global perspective, we should understand that educated women are healthier, have fewer and appropriately-spaced children, and are more likely to rise out of poverty. The benefits extend to better outcomes for the children, who will be less likely to be exploited, and who will themselves have a greater chance at health and education. This further extends to greater environmental health and the potential for greater psychological and societal flourishing. Please see Alan Weisman's, *Countdown: Our Last, Best Hope for a Future on Earth,* for a full, relevant, and uncomfortable discussion on these issues.

A Christian Ethic for the Modern Church

We must abandon and renounce the "prosperity gospel," which is no gospel at all. We must deconstruct and abandon the cult of celebrity among Christian ministers. Let us not support the jets and the mansions. Let us defund this darkness against Jesus' body. We do this by direct speech and action, by leaving an organization if needed, and by being intentional with our dollars. We refuse to participate in manipulative forms of "ministry." We take God at his Word, that there is a priesthood of believers, and challenge the psychology that says a massive organization is needed to establish spiritual authority. Maybe we can give some of these building complexes to our municipalities to use for convention centers or offices, along with a note of apology. This pandemic may be the first of many trials that will come upon the whole earth. We are certainly facing the declining state of the earth itself, the growing population, the aging infrastructure, the untenability of the world's current regimen of consumption, the illusions of many of our sustainable green energy initiatives, the loss of species and habitat, the growing scarcity of precious metals and materials for our technological products (which are already indispensable to us), economic contraction and unbelievable corruption. This sad list could also be extended forever. This nation is changing. This is not alarmism. It is reality. It is upon us now. One author suggested that maybe the world won't end tomorrow, but it *will* change. As stated, we need not embrace the idea that we can and must "fix" the world, but we do need to develop a more holistic response to the world in light of our modern realities.

The Church must be the bearers of God's truth. We begin by getting our own house in order. We display the integrity of those who are doers of the Word and not hearers only. This world is tending toward confusion, hopelessness, and

A Proposed Organizational Ethic Drawn from Several Sources

emptiness for so many. The Church has the answers to the human condition, but we must be living and true epistles if we are to have any real impact.

We have discussed several practical and psychological changes that we might consider at the organizational level. Next, we will proceed into a practical ethic for us as individuals, connecting it with all that has been discussed.

8

A PROPOSED PERSONAL ETHIC DRAWN FROM SEVERAL SOURCES

By this we may know we are in him: whoever says he abides in him ought to walk the same way in which he walked (1 John 2:5b-6).

See also: Isaiah 58, Acts 10:38, Amos 5, Micah 6:8, 1 Pet 2:5,9,21, 1 Cor 3:12, 15:58, Eph 2:10, Phil 2:5,7, Lu 2:49, Jn 4:34, 18:37.

Our first consideration in the development of a proposed personal ethic is the *recovery of a unified ultimate and proximate meaning in Christ that will inform our lives and practice.* Jesus came to this earth on a mission. We are here for specific reasons. God has a mission for each of us, and if we are in denial of this fact, we will spend our lives building structures of wood, hay, and stubble, as the Scripture says. This is a real terror, even in light of the sovereignty of God. 1 Corinthians 3:12-15 is a dire warning, but it is also a word that holds great promise. We would ask ourselves what constitutes a meaningful life, without constructing an ideology that amounts to yet another burden.

We are already overwhelmed! The gospel is the promise of freedom. See John 8:36. So, if we hold the Scripture to be the rule of faith and practice, we are forced to wonder why so many are disconnected from this true freedom.

Maslow and the idea of self-actualization is one standard teaching concerning human beings' source of meaning and the aim of our greatest good in Western thought. The idea is proliferated throughout psychology, sociology, and management. I might suggest the idea of transcendence *contra* Maslow, and I would not be the first, although some would argue that transcendence is but one manifestation of self-actualization. In American Western thought, we have embraced a "rugged individualism," which, I would submit, is one harmful facet of the idea of self-actualization in that it has resulted in the loss of intimate social structure. As a result of the idealization of the individual, we see not a liberation, but devastating isolation of the individual from the types of endeavor and relationships that would allow for intimate belonging and expression. This is what we so often seek in distorted ways in overwork, in bars, on social media, and in an infinity of dark, lonely holes with our compulsive behaviors and addictions. How much of our violent crime and mental illness could be traced back to these myriad unmet needs and dysfunctional societal structures? How many professing Christians are addicted to substances and pornography? To overwork? To political outrage? To the numbing effects of media distraction, having resigned in some measure to a life

A Proposed Personal Ethic Drawn from Several Sources

short of significant meaning and endeavor, even when we cannot articulate it?

Christianity has often promoted a psychology of self-denial that few people can flourish in, and by some definitions, it would seem to fall short of the full intention of the Christian message. Even Jesus said that those of us who lose our lives for his sake will *find* them. Many people have found Christianity to be a suffocating burden, and at this point in history, they are leaving the Church and/or the faith altogether. Contrariwise, much of American "Christendom" has embraced mammon as the intended expression of the gospel, ". . . supposing that gain is godliness" (1 Tim 6:5).

In another vein, we might consider the damaging effects of a Christianity devoid of any constraint or responsibility, which is no Christianity at all. We would hope to see a renewal of Christianity that is *full* of meaning and life-giving practice, including a robust morality, and a level of ownership that is appropriate to each of us.

There are manifold factors that contribute to the phenomena mentioned. However, is it possible that reintegrating Christian people with meaningful ministry and relationship, restoring an eschatological reality that encompasses our now *and* our not yet, developing a holistic understanding of our place in the created order with all that flows from that, and seeking simplicity during our modern chaos would begin to promote Christian wholeness and fulfillment by all the metrics we have mentioned?

Viktor Frankl observed that even within the horrors of the prison camps during the second world war, certain individuals were, "able to retreat from their terrible surroundings to a life of inner riches and spiritual freedom."[1] These are people who have devoted an effective portion of their finite time in this world to develop their inner lives. They had spent the energies necessary to carry within themselves deep wells of spiritual knowledge and experience. It is without a doubt that we receive input constantly in life. Much of that input, as we have discussed, has been carefully engineered by someone else to very specific ends. What portion of our time, resources, attention, and very psychological framework is captive to the devices of the internet, the entertainment industry, the news networks, and the cult of mammon?

Lest we should seem too ethereal, we must also include the development of important relationships and experiences that form a meaningful core to our *curriculum vitae,* and not think that spiritual depth and value are developed by just reading a lot of books or practicing asceticism.

Most important in this endeavor is the time spent with our Father. It is he that nourishes us by his very presence and Word, by the supply of his Spirit, and by the intercession of the Son. See Phil 1:19, Heb 7:25, Rev 2:5, Rev 3:18. It is in this place of prayer and communion that we are changed, that we are filled with God's presence. See Paul's prayer for the Ephesians in the third chapter, verses 14-21. We are availed of strength, faith, agape, comprehension, of intimate knowledge of the love of Christ. Mary sat at his feet and heard his word. See Luke 10:39. Jesus resorted frequently to prayer, alone with his Father. See Luke 5:16, 9:28. We must enter the terrifying silence, the *mysterium tremendum* of God. This is the only proper posture and locus of the professing Christian. Francis Schaeffer observes, "Without the infinite personal God, man can only make systems."[2] We, however, want to participate in life and the community, the purposes of God, in true meaning and fulfillment, to obey the greatest commandment.

A Proposed Personal Ethic Drawn from Several Sources

So, how does this bear out day to day? It first means the deliberate pursuit of God through prayer and worship in their several forms. And our definitions of prayer and worship are so narrow! I have endured untold guilt in church worship services.

So often songs were not resonating with me, and the formulaic nature of the worship service felt contrived. Conversely, I have been blown away while watching a flock of birds go by, a deer in the forest, a campfire, and an octopus. I have watched a video of a Dutch choir singing *Agnus Dei* about a million times now, and I weep every time. I have scarce been able to get the words out from trembling and weeping, when I have been able to help hand out the communion elements, "This is the body of Christ, broken *for you.*" For you. In that moment, we are surrounded by the presence of the risen Jesus Christ, filled with his Spirit, and loved by his Father. We are observers, participants (to be so bold) of that mysterious exchange mediated by the love of God. His love for my sin. His substance for my emptiness. In this place, the bitter and contrived strifes and dramas of this world lose meaning. Can we see it?

So we pray without ceasing. We worship. We meditate on what God has done for us. We practice gratitude in concrete ways, whether by giving, time, presence with others, or service. We pray for eyes to see and a heart to understand. We learn the discipline of silence, where the illusion of our self-sufficiency is allowed to melt away into God's true sufficiency, where the need to control the narrative, to work, worry, and do ourselves to death is allowed to die. Did not God tell us that his discipline leaves us with the "peaceable fruit of righteousness?" (Heb 12:11). Let us enter into the truth of Isaiah 30:15, "For thus saith the LORD God, the Holy One of Israel; in returning and rest shall ye be saved; in quietness and in confidence shall be your strength . . ." Hebrews 4:9-10 explains, "So then, there remains a Sabbath rest for the people of God, for whoever has entered God's rest has also rested from his works as God did from his." Learn the complete sentence of, "No."

Time spent with God does what is impossible by other means. It changes our hearts and priorities. It alleviates fears and anxieties. It shapes our desire. It relieves our anger and insecurity. It fills our emptiness. Our earthly communion with God is the shadowy foretaste of that for which he has purchased us.

I recommend Richard Foster's, *Celebration of Discipline*. Drawn from a deep well of Agape and experience, it is a practical guide on the reason, the means, and the methods for individual and corporate engagement with God.

It is easy to translate all of this into what we call "quiet time" in our modern parlance. I hope we will consider a broader perspective. In Western thought, the emphasis is so often placed on individual self-sufficiency. While we cannot deny that time alone with God is vital, I would also add that much of our spiritual nourishment and fellowship with God can and should be carried out communally. I am thinking of communities of people who all have their "boots on the ground," so to speak. This is what we seek to develop as we challenge the ethos of the Institution. When each of us has taken *ownership* of our call to the Gospel, our prayer time is different. Our major concerns are different. There is a quality of fellowship that is deeper than what is often found in consumer churches.

We have talked here again about prayer and communion with God. Our earlier chapter on prayer focused more on the

A Proposed Personal Ethic Drawn from Several Sources

"activist" facet of prayer, that of prayer as the fundamental action of the Christian. Here, in contrast, we have focused more on the relational aspect. Hopefully, between the two I have shared some helpful and practical suggestions for a more robust and satisfying engagement in prayer.

One caveat is in order. It is easy to talk in big, swelling words about prayer and spiritual ecstasy, but the Scripture and experience bear out that it is a labor of faith. The dark night of the soul is a reality. The dry times and disappointments are realities. Gethsemane is a reality. The waiting, whether on answers to prayer or fruitfulness in ministry, is a reality. So are the manifold difficulties of "life in community." With that in mind, I hope we will be persistent in prayer, good works, and face-to-face love of real people.

Next, let us consider how we can fill our souls with good spiritual food. Reading the Bible and Christian classics are givens for most of us, even when discipline seems hard to come by. What can we also learn by broadening our experience with classic and world literature, for example? For each of us, how can we deepen and fill the well Dr. Frankl mentioned, both with knowledge and experience? What role does frank obedience to Jesus and the scripture play in the development of a meaningful life? What would happen if we spent non-judgmental time with people, face to face and listening, with whom we have profound disagreements, whether they be political, moral, or otherwise? What about people who are different from us by way of race, nationality, or religion? Jesus was a man among the people, and we cannot minister to others competently unless we know them. Who knows what others have to teach us as well!

Much of our internal turmoil, I am convinced, stems from our spiritual malnourishment. We simply do not have a sufficient intake of positive, nutrient-dense experience, knowledge, and relationship to keep us healthy.

We have talked at length in this work about where we have gotten it wrong; should we not also learn about the rich history of all that the Church has contributed to this world? It is good to get an accurate understanding of the impact of Christ's appearance on the world in the historic sense, and how his revelation gave all of humanity the power and promise for healing and significant reform of institutions. In addition, Jesus gave us a renewed understanding of what humanity *is*. All the seeds of justice and equality of humans before God were planted in Christ and confirmed in his resurrection. If that were not enough, Jesus' resurrection is the promise of restoration for the entire cosmos. It is the promise of present power and eternal life. We are invited to not only learn but to participate in this history.

Continuing, we consider our relationship to the negative inputs, that spiritual junk food, in our lives, whether that is TV, social media, mainstream media, or whatever. I am not advocating a life of asceticism or ignorance, but I am advocating an active engagement in spiritual health, which will extend into every area of our lives.

Without these being the active principles in our lives, our reality is of necessity the illusion. It is the chaos and perpetual outrage of the news channels and social media. It is the ceaseless and dehumanizing violence of the utilitarian construct as manifested in our workplaces, our epidemic levels of stress, and perceived responsibility. It is the absence of meaning that is evidenced in our drug epidemics and suicide, (which I have witnessed with my own eyes again and again, and with which I have struggled in my own life) in the desperate grasping after "causes" and "identities" that

A Proposed Personal Ethic Drawn from Several Sources

consumes our young people. God's people must understand that when rightly ordered, causes and identities proceed from God. When the cause is itself a person's only source of meaning, as in the case of so much of our current activism, there can be no true fulfillment. There can only be a desperate striving to win. There is no vital principle. When the cause fails, I fail. When the cause dies, I die, so to speak. There is a loss of identity, which has become the precious, ill-defined commodity of our young people. This is one reason for the manifestation of violence in much of our society's activism. It is the same reason that church programs in isolation from a vital corporate relationship with God are so dangerous and tragic.

Having taken a brief look at some "internal" considerations for the Christian, we proceed to consider a second necessity in the development of a personal ethic. Romans 13:10 captures the idea in succinct words, "Love does no wrong to a neighbor, therefore, love is the fulfilling of the law."

Let us contemplate verse 9 of the same chapter, "For the commandments, 'You shall not commit adultery, You shall not murder, You shall not steal, You shall not covet,' and any other commandment, are summed up in this word: 'You shall love your neighbor as yourself.'" Look at this short list of specific transgressions and for a moment lay that against the practices of corporations and big government, environmentally destructive industries, traffickers of human beings, and such as we have discussed. How have our consumption habits diminished us and contributed to human exploitation? Consider the fact that we still need lots of immigrants for cheap labor in our unpalatable yet "indispensable" industries right here in America. Consider the millions of factory-farmed animals. How about our mindless production of plastic waste? Of all waste! Of our excessive use of power and stuff? See again James 5:1-6.

Consider the wantonness and sheer tragedy of our war-making machine, the reality of which is unconscionable, and which has been twisted in the public consciousness as something our Lord Jesus is rooting for and approves of. While there may have been at times just causes, I submit that many of our military interventions have been at root little more than the preservation of our satanic economic program, or misguided initiatives of politicians who *need* war, who sell us war because war is a sense of power and the movement of unimaginable amounts of money. Our young men and women are being killed and devastated physically and psychologically at the whim of our political-economic machine and our excess consumption. There are few American people indeed who are willing to take an honest and circumspect look at the history of our military behavior good, bad, and ugly. Perhaps among Christians, we could make an honest assessment, and allow that to influence our praxis and our rhetoric. Jimmy Carter once called the US the "most warlike nation in the history of the world." https://www.counterpunch.org/2019/04/19/jimmy-carter-us-most-warlike-nation-in-history-of-the-world/ accessed October 5, 2021. The article goes on to state that there have been only *five* years of our 242 years of existence that have been without war, attack, or occupation. Those were the years of President Carter's term, and the year previous. It continues by outlining how far behind we are in infrastructure and technology due to our war-making, and the incredible costs involved. To take a minute portion of our military spending and apply it to those issues, we could have high-speed rails. We could update our infrastructure

A Proposed Personal Ethic Drawn from Several Sources

and have change to spare. We could address our inequitable and corrupt healthcare system. We could address poverty and our failing educational systems. Tragically, this is our reality. Many American citizens understand this according to polls. As the Christian Church, we would do well to understand. Many social issues could be ameliorated by promoting more accountability in our government, and by promoting accurate knowledge among the people of God. Where can we be on the front lines of these changes? At this phase of empire, I would suggest that local, grassroots activism is more likely to bring about significant change. When great numbers of people withdraw support from wicked systems and develop healthy local systems in any given domain, positive change is inevitable, but it requires numbers, education, labor, and consistent pressure.

Thoreau lamented long ago in his tract, "On the Duty of Civil Disobedience," that a soldier acting in concert with his conscience is by definition an act of treason. They are not allowed to decide what is just or unjust in the taking of human life, the occupation of foreign lands, and the destruction of others' property and livelihood. Can we consider the history of aggression of Great Britain and the United States against the oil-producing nations, our proxy wars with Russia in Afghanistan, the effects of CIA meddling in central and south America, the Spanish-American War in which we killed over a million *Filipinos*, the war with Mexico (the reason for the writing of Thoreau's tract) in which we committed atrocities against the Mexican people, the wars in Korea and Viet Nam, where the justification for our presence is suspect at best, and the bombing of middle east nations at the behest of our administration to put attention off of political scandals? The list goes on and on, and the subject of America's military-

A Christian Ethic for the Modern Church

industrial complex is so volatile, that it is often impossible to discuss. But, as Christians whose metric is supposed to be in line with the teachings of Jesus, we would do well to evaluate how we think about these issues, and how we present ourselves to others. Blessed are the peacemakers, Jesus said, and not so much blessed are the warmongers. We are called to be ambassadors for Christ, imploring others to be reconciled to God. We have a major imperative. Where is the space for belligerence toward other nations?

All of this being said, it is necessary to be understanding of our warfighters. An incredible amount of camaraderie, community and proximate meaning often take place in the experience of war and military service. Our military personnel often help many people. They cling to their experiences and take pride in their service. The vast majority of them, I believe, are good-hearted people who want to serve their country, defend freedom, and take out bad guys. As a people, we need to take care of our veterans. At the same time, however, we understand that warfare is destructive to our people. We look at the impact in terms of PTSD, untold emotional suffering of veterans and their families, disabilities, and epidemic levels of suicide. As Christians, I believe that supporting our veterans *and* calling for an end to war are not conflicting objectives.

While it seems like I have contradicted myself in talking so much about things "out there" when I am trying to suggest an ethic for the Church, there is a reason for this. We have a bearing on it all, whether for good or ill. Likewise, it is too easy to dismiss personal responsibility by shaking our heads at institutions or the "sad state of things." Impact begins with personal ownership and action. Each of us must do something. Understanding this is the beginning of our being

A Proposed Personal Ethic Drawn from Several Sources

able to change, to "come out and be separate." Ephesians 5:11-13, 15-17 states, "Take no part in the unfruitful works of darkness, but instead expose them. For it is shameful even to speak of the things that they do in secret. But when anything is exposed to the light, it becomes visible... Look carefully then how you walk, not as unwise, but as wise, making the best use of the time, because the days are evil. Therefore do not be foolish, but understand what the will of the Lord is."

An individual ethic of innocence and simplicity would alleviate much of the harm we cause, even when we do not mean to. As Christians, we must take seriously God's second great commandment to work no ill to our neighbor. And our neighbor is *everyone*. When I became an EMT seventeen years ago or so, I learned the first rule of medicine, "First, do no harm." *Primum non nocere*. It is the constant and careful assessment of my actions and their consequences on the people I am charged to treat. As Christians in the modern church, in an affluent society, in a declining earth, in a bitterly divided polity, we must make this *thorough* assessment at the individual, personal level. Where and how do *I* cause harm? How has wantonness or ignorance degraded me spiritually, and psychologically? How have my consumption habits affected workers overseas, my local economy, and the environment? How does my lifestyle contribute to ecological devastation, human exploitation, to the perpetuation of wicked industries and systems? How has the spirit of this age and my political behavior fomented classism, racism, or the diminishment or outright ignorance of the "other," whether next door or around the world? How can I be a part of diminishing the need for the war-making machine? What is my attitude toward the physical materials that pass through my hands and into the trash daily, the usable metals, and paper, the single-use plastic, the food waste, and the hoardes of personal possessions? As a first responder who has been in thousands of homes, and as an observer of open garage doors, I can testify that we have taken way more than our share of this world's resources. We have done it to our own hurt. So many of us cannot even access the majority of our personal possessions! Why? Didn't Jesus tell us that our lives do not consist in the abundance of the things which we possess? Didn't the apostle Paul state that it is certain we can take nothing out of this world when we leave? They are talking to us.

I contend that the development of the internal spiritual life as discussed before will alleviate much of this need to hoard and consume. We must ask other questions as well. What will I leave in my wake? What will be the mark of my passing through this world? A garage full of stuff? Is it possible to leave a spiritual hoard behind? If there is a crisis of meaning in the Church that leads to all of this, we are of all people the most miserable, and the light of God is growing dim indeed for this world.

Let us pursue with abandon an ethos of innocence and simplicity. Let us follow Jesus' admonition to the rich young ruler. Read Matthew 19:16-25. The man in the story, no doubt was a godly man who was mindful of the commandments of God, but Jesus struck at the heart of the man's malady. He was possessed by that which he possessed. What was Jesus' remedy? Get rid of it. Give to the poor and follow me. And look at the exchange! Jesus offered the man an incorruptible treasure in heaven, an objectively real, and far superior hoard. He offered the man relationship and purpose for the *now* also. See v 21. What true riches have we forfeited!

A Proposed Personal Ethic Drawn from Several Sources

I once worked through a process in David Allen's book, *Getting Things Done*. Down to the last nut, bolt, rubber band, sock, receipt, thumb tack, tool, book, and pencil, I went through *every single thing* I owned, some things I had not touched in years. There were things I did not remember owning. There was trash, literal trash, in drawers, on shelves, in closets. There were mounds of things neither beautiful nor useful, clothes I'd never wear, tools and materials I would never use, books I would never read. It seemed endless! The reality of all of this is that our hoards, our unfinished projects, and our *stuff* all takes up mental and spiritual real estate. Jesus said, "Where your treasure is, there will your heart be also."

So, I began to build and assign piles: trash, give, thrift store, garage sale. I began to do the same with my intangible responsibilities, everything: do it right now, drop it, defer it, delegate it, everything out of one's head, and assigned a definite end.

I cleared out my life and my mind. When the initial process was completed, I sat down and wept. There was a tangible catharsis, a lifting of the burden. (It has been suggested that the fallacy in our productivity systems in America is that we are only trying to become more efficient at doing a never-ending number of things when what we might strive for is doing the few most meaningful things with our full attention.) What weight are we carrying in our society? Have we challenged the ways of the world, that we must always be busy? That we must do every youth activity and sport, every church function, every social event? That we must work ourselves to death during the healthiest years of our lives so that when we are old, sick, and stressed we can retire and "take our leisure?" Is the main thrust of our lives living the gospel and doing the will of God, or the relentless demands of modern life?

A Christian Ethic for the Modern Church

Likewise, have we cleaned out our spiritual houses? I have looked at consumer*ism* thus far from more of a physical standpoint, but what about the wounds we bear as human beings? Some of us have been so traumatized by abuses, assaults, terrible family dynamics, abandonment, the world, poverty, and lack, in short by life, that we have grasped at the rudiments of this world in a desperate attempt to find some measure of control and safety. Can we seek wholeness in Christ and fellowship with other people? Can we be available to others for *their* healing? I believe that the very availability of ourselves for relationships *is* the beginning of healing.

Let us keep in mind that we do not know what other people have been through. How many times over the decades of my life have I returned to those "weak and beggarly elements?" Some people have such deep wounds that it may be the work of a lifetime for them to trust in God and find spiritual healing. Indeed, it may be part and parcel of the communal Christian experience, that we may all learn the patience and commitment Christ seeks to develop in us. See Romans 15:1 on bearing with the weak. My own experience with the sheer demoralizing entrenchment of mental illness and addiction demonstrates the pressing need in the Church for us to simply, faithfully, and consistently *love each other*. So often, our modern church experience, with its need for efficiency, with our impatience and busyness, with our preaching of wealth or the "therapeutic" psychology that puts an oasis of no suffering just out of reach, is but salt in the open wound. It is a foreign language to the sufferer. I submit that this is why so many "fall through the cracks" in the industrial church.

We must treat people according to where they are. We must have mercy upon them and ourselves. We must recover

A Proposed Personal Ethic Drawn from Several Sources

a proper theology of suffering. Indeed, we could make that another chapter, another book! Let us move forward, and let us remember that we are not meant to do this alone. Let us avail ourselves of community, and of every help that is out there. Spiritual mentors, therapists, groups, friends, family, community, recreation, art, writing, medical help, a healthy lifestyle, reading, service, self-care, and nature. Be a person who is available to others in the ministry of *presence and listening*.

The third consideration in the development of a personal Christian ethic is the wise and compassionate use of wealth in accordance with the nature of God and in continuance of our second principle of "working no ill" to one's neighbor. Whether we agree with all of our history, ways, and means, we are the most affluent nation on earth. That may be changing soon, as China is making nearly everything, and they do not spend a fraction of what we spend militarily. Other factors go into why this may soon be the case, but nevertheless, the Church in America has a unique imperative. As we turn our hearts and minds away from "rugged individualism," industrial, consumer church, and the pursuit of wealth for wealth's sake, we are in a position to consider how to use our resources in concert with a Christlike mode of life.

If we are going to go to a brick-and-mortar church, I believe it is good to support it, but I believe that the "ten percent to the local church" mandate is a contrivance of man, and not in accordance with the Scripture, especially in light of the church's current use of it, as we have discussed. The new covenant tells us to give as God has enabled us. See 1 Cor 16:2. Second Corinthians 9:6f teaches us the psychology of giving. We are to be generous givers because he will not fail to provide for us. We can get away from the strictures of this tithe mentality by being generous within an intimate community and toward others in need. Seeing our money and resources help someone firsthand is one of the surest ways to become a joyful giver. It is not about checking off the ten percent box. It is about *becoming*. Becoming a giver. Jesus tells us it is more blessed to give than to receive. See Acts 20:35. The beauty of this is that when it is about the identity and nature of the human being and our communities, even those we consider "poor" can become a part of the sharing community, as opposed to constant recipients. We can perhaps begin to undo the self-defeating psychology of poverty. It is an increase of joy and meaning for all of us.

We should be gracious as we teach new believers about giving. In the institutional setting, it can be very cold and manipulative. We want to adopt people into a community of love where there is a mutual ethos of sharing, not into an institution that takes your money. This has been a perennial criticism from those outside the Church, and it has not been helped by our celebrity "ministers" living in mansions and flying in private jets all over. Those who are able should work at something, for their own spiritual, psychological, and physical health, as well as for relieving the Church of the burden so that they can help others, and so that person "may have to give to him who needs" See Eph 4:28.

As individuals, we can become informed and deliberate about where our money goes. That means in the church and our spending habits. Do not support church debt or excessive or irresponsible use of money. Our home church model has freed up our giving to near one hundred percent for meal sharing and *direct* compassionate ministry to people in need.

A Proposed Personal Ethic Drawn from Several Sources

We might consider not supporting parachurch organizations whose model is paternalistic, or who subvert the role of parents in poor nations to generate pity by showcasing the children only. Let us support the holistic, practical assistance of families or whole communities, without manipulative marketing. Please don't misunderstand. Many of these organizations are doing amazing work but let us challenge the method when we need to.

In our money mindfulness, let us also consider being non-consumers when possible. What about the more radical decisions to downsize houses and possessions? Do we support local businesses and resist the purchase of foreign-made goods whenever possible? Besides just being the right thing to do in my opinion, in large enough numbers, these types of activities have the potential to change communities and institutions, to change the mindset of communities. In the bargain, we may win people to Christ by being "globally conscious," and community-minded.

On even more practical levels, what about buying reusable cups, straws, shopping bags, and produce bags? Bring your leftover dish to the restaurant? Forgoing straws, lids, and excess packaging, and finding alternatives to single-use items wherever possible. Eat at home. Eat local, humanely raised and slaughtered, pasture-raised meats. Eat non-big ag produce, preferably grown nearby, or by yourself. If there is no local "food shed," what about being instrumental in its development? By eating healthy, local foods we reduce our participation not only in those poisonous big foods but in the medical and pharmaceutical industries as well. We also reduce fossil fuel usage in many cases. It is a win-win-win. Every one of these decisions weakens the power of those industries that perpetuate exploitation, our sickness, and the degradation of our humanity. When the destruction of myth occurs, the potential to build something better becomes reality.

But alas, God's people yet have a higher purpose. We are not going to usher in Utopia, but we may be able to cause substantial healing for many. We may be able to cause significant change, and in so doing, we are a light to the lost of the goodness of God and gospel. We are being the stewards of our Lord's property, and being transformed into his image in the process. God will judge Babylon fully in his time, but for now, we are to "come out of her, that [we] be not partaker of her plagues" (Rom 18:4, KJV). This is where the correct eschatological understanding comes in.

It is by the general revelation of God in his creation, the Word of God, the revelation of God to humanity through the incarnation of Jesus and all that he did, and by the abiding presence of his Church and Spirit during this age that God will judge the world. See Rom 1:20. I have heard it said that a good God must be a God of judgment. The universalist theology that is becoming a mainstay in Western Christianity has not come to grips with the nature of evil, or the depths of human cruelty that is again, not the aberration but our fallen nature itself. It has twisted and denied the Scriptural narrative. Jesus did not purchase tacit approval for the works of Satan and wicked humanity. See Acts 17:30-31. He has purchased a People. Whosoever will. Evil is still evil, and God "commands everyone who names the name of Christ to depart from iniquity" (2 Tim 2:19).

The first thing that anyone notices who has tried to live innocently, fairly, and humanely, to "do no harm," is the sheer difficulty of it. Doubtless, we need certain things to live. We have to go to work. We need food, clothing, and shelter.

A Proposed Personal Ethic Drawn from Several Sources

Sometimes we need a vacation, God knows! What I am talking about is a paradigm shift. We can all start somewhere and do something, but let it be persistent, deliberate, and significant. 1 Corinthians 7:30-31 states in the KJV, "... and they that buy, as though they possessed not; And they that use this world, as not abusing *it*: for the fashion of this world passeth away."

Imagine a thousand-member congregation agreeing to buy canvas or hemp grocery bags this Sunday. Put the church logo on them, and let everyone buy them at a markup. The proceeds could be used to support a ministry project. Let us suppose that each person bought one, and they were saved from using just one plastic bag a week; that is fifty-two thousand bags per year not in the landfill, the ocean, or the incinerator. Fifty-two thousand advertisements for your church. Fifty-two thousand times you get to say, "We care about what God has made. We care about you." This is sharing the gospel message through the ethos of stewardship. This is one tiny, hypothetical, simple action that could build cohesiveness among the body and have a literal impact. What if the entire American church got in on this type of "activism?" What if God's church here became known as this giant organism of people who *care?* People who care about the world we live in, and the people in it, who eschew the allurements of money, power, and discrimination? What if we all around became the kind of people who live in innocence, simplicity, and spiritual depth?

It is astounding how this change of mindset can free us. And, it is an additive effect. As we progress in a life of simplicity, we begin to understand the tremendous weight of our stuff, the stress it causes, and the mental real estate it takes up. New rest and inspiration begin to open up within us. I can testify to this firsthand. Likewise, when we begin to view our money, commodities, and possessions as gifts of our God who provides for us, and we enter a life of extravagant giving and sharing, we will discover not only a release from the nagging anxiety of scarcity, but also joy, meaning, and purpose as we see community form, needs met, people healed internally-*because we gave*. This is not theory; it is God's word to us, and it will bear out in our lives.

Having developed an ethos of spiritual depth, innocence, and simplicity, having freed ourselves from the clutches of "stuff," and the non-compassionate use of wealth, it is incumbent on every professing Christian to be *directly* involved in some kind of relational service, ministry, and/or activism. This is our fourth consideration.

There is a very specific principle at work here that I think bears extrapolation. First, it is always easier to drop a check in the mail, have perfect Sunday attendance, or even consistently practice certain habits like Bible reading, than to get involved with messy people and situations. This may be a fundamental malady of the modern Church, the substitution of religious exercise for true Agape love. Brennan Manning observes that "[m]inimal investment in propriety and good deeds yields the rewards of the faith community, adulation and praise. The appeal of hypocrisy is powerful."[3]

Matthew 25:31-46 relates the well-known story of the sheep and the goats. It is important to look at this parable not as a checklist of activities that will win us God's favor, but as a metric of our heart, and the animating principle within us. And what is the acid test of how we have related to Jesus? How we have related to the "least of these." In Luke 10, the lawyer asked Jesus, "And who is my neighbor?" The fact that

A Proposed Personal Ethic Drawn from Several Sources

he had to ask that question in the first place is indicative of a deep-down soul sickness that can afflict all of us, and even more so in an affluent society with large, shiny church productions.

We have constructed a vast framework in our society for the sole purpose of feeling spiritually good while avoiding our neighbors. Church programs, busyness, the sanctification of the marketplace, our institution of (ungodly expensive) "religious" education, and even nationalism and patriotism have contributed in perverse ways to making us feel "alright" before God.

Jesus commands us to anoint our blind eyes with salve, so we may see. Ellul says, "Rediscover your neighbor through the Holy Spirit," that we must develop a "[w]ill to find objective reality. To discover the facts of the people around me, [to] grasp this reality on the human level, forgoing ideal, abstraction, and future, [to] stop thinking of "men," and start thinking of my neighbor, 'Mario.'"[4]

Manning continues in desperation, "Everything is at stake. The hour is late. We are called not to fear, but to action."[5]

We have discussed the first commandment, loving God with all our heart, soul, mind, and strength. Everything since has been in the interest of fulfilling the second great commandment to love our neighbor as ourselves. Those discussions, up to this point, have been largely passive, concerned with "coming out of," or a refusal to participate in, those things that cause further harm. Now we arrive at the active principle of direct ministry. Being isolated from active engagement with the true community, and face-to-face ministry is degenerative to our spiritual vitality. It is a stagnant pool with no outlet. In the insular spiritual society, we may put our faith in our intellect and theological knowledge.

A Christian Ethic for the Modern Church

We may tend to create a paranoid outer world of bogeymen to be vilified. We could become smug in our religious standing. Many people have experienced a profound loss of meaning. Perhaps we develop a whole lot of programs and activities that have little impact on the greater good, or they reproduce unhealthy models. For many, many of us in the West, it is the pursuit of wealth that prevents us from a full life in Christ.

When we meet the real needs of individual people, when we engage face to face, our religious pretensions, our hatreds and prejudices, our political posturing, our arrogance, loneliness, and emptiness, all have the opportunity to die, to be swallowed up in the love of Christ, and in the fellowship of his Spirit. There is relief in this. How many of us need this! In addition, real people are experiencing the love and gospel of Jesus.

That being said, it is not easy.

This is a brief and inadequate meditation on the development of a Christian ethic, but I trust that it is sufficient to ignite humble reflection within the Body of Christ and the individual Christian. The hour is late and the need is great for God's beacon to shine at its brightest. The world is being tried. Confusion abounds. Judgment begins at the house of God. We need a significant renewal movement in our Church. The generations coming after us need to see God's people at work remedying the excesses, abuses, and distortions of our past. If they are paying any heed at all to the Church, I imagine many feel they have been handed the check for a party they did not attend, and which destroyed the house.

In our final section, "The Agape Feast," we will consider that holy place, "whither the forerunner is for us entered, even

A Proposed Personal Ethic Drawn from Several Sources

Jesus," (Heb 6:20, KJV) the place where the veil was torn from top to bottom, laying bare the very heart of God. I pray that you may be affected, healed, and surrounded by the love and community of God, "And to know the love of Christ, which passes knowledge, that ye might be filled with all the fullness of God" (Eph 3:19, KJV).

9
THE AGAPE FEAST

I have related the events of our first few years back in town, our poverty, my father's seizures, my mother's traumatic pregnancies, and my sense of social rejection in the church and at school. I have recounted my church and life experiences from childhood and forward. I would now like to recount another event, but I would like to ask each of us to pause and truly enter into our experience. I would like us to consider for a moment, how we feel, and how others might feel. So often we hear stories, but how often do we enter into another person's experience? At what level have we entered into and reckoned with our own experience? Have we made space for and sat with our reality? For many of us, the battle to avoid our pain has cost us dearly in myriad ways, lost or damaged relationships, substance abuse, mental illness and isolation, loneliness, dissociation, depression and anxiety, and a thousand compulsions. It is only as we face our own experiences, that we avail ourselves of the possibility of healing. We can have permission here to say, "That sucked, and I don't understand it." In addition, we become able to develop understanding and empathy. We *re-humanize* the other. We validate the other. This is the beginning of the end of isolation and the utilitarian mind. It is the beginning of healing in a defined sense, the rejoining of that which has been broken. Let us keep this thought in mind as we proceed.

During one dreary Christmas season, amid our several troubles, our house was robbed. Someone had gone through all our Christmas gifts under the tree, torn them apart, and taken what they wanted. Needless to say, it was a frightening and demoralizing experience.

One Sunday after this incident, a large box appeared in the church foyer with our family's name on it. There was no indication as to who it was from. We got the box home to find it stuffed with Christmas gifts, several for each of us. Among the gifts I received was a Walkman cassette player/radio with headphones. I cannot describe the elation I felt seeing those gifts. The Walkman instantly became a prized possession carrying with it the gift of music, a gift that has saved my life and my sanity many times since, even that *rock music*.

The real gift in that box was Agape. It was compassion. It was the heart that saw a need and took action. Galatians 5:6 reminds us that the active principle in "religion" is "faith that works by love." In a brief digression, I would just like to mention again that the futility of our religious observance is the offense of the cross. The prettier we make ourselves, the harder we try to be "good" Christians, often turns out to be the degree to which we resist the grace of God. Didn't Jesus lament over Jerusalem, "how often I would have gathered your children together, even as a hen gathers her chicks under her wings, and ye would not" (Mt 23:37, KJV). Let us again stop and meditate. Did not God create Adam in his own image? And we know that Eve was drawn from him. All that we inadequately define as masculine and feminine were

The Agape Feast

bound up in this protohuman, created in the image of God. And here we see Jesus baring his solicitude, his vulnerability, his *motherhood,* in the analogy of a hen, wings extended that her chicks may run under and into safety. (cf Psalm 91:4, Deut 32:11, Is 66:13, Is 49:15, 1 Thess 2:7, Gal 4:19, Gal 3:28, Hosea 13:8, Deut 32:18, Lu 15:8-10, Is 42:14, Hos 11:1-4)

A distinct theme began to emerge as I recounted my forty-plus years' experience in church. The times I felt loved and connected involved the sharing of meals and this world's goods, whether I was the sharer or the "share-ee." The Biblical precedent for this is pervasive and deceptively simple. The most oft-quoted verses on this "topic" (an unfortunate word for what we are discussing) are those found in Acts 2:44-47, KJV, "And all that believed were together, and had all things common; and sold their possessions and goods, and parted them to all men, as every man had need. And they, continuing daily with one accord in the temple, and breaking bread from house to house, did eat their meat with gladness and singleness of heart, praising God, and having favour with all the people. And the Lord added to the church daily such as should be saved." See also Acts 4:29-37. For those of us familiar with the popular "Love Languages" idea, we can see that in this community, they are all spoken. The charge here is to go and do likewise. It is possible to live like this.

Luke 24:35 relates to us that Jesus was "known" in the breaking of bread. Jesus said also, "He that eats my flesh and drinks my blood, dwells in me, and I in him. As the living Father has sent me, and I live by the Father: so he that eateth me, even he shall live by me" (John 6:56-57, KJV). It is the mysterious reality we experience, which we enter into in the celebration of the Eucharist, the communion. I grew up with a "low" view of communion, and there are well thought out arguments for the major views, but as I have gotten older I have begun to see that this meal, this fellowship, is representative of the very heart of God, of the nature of the Godhead "it" self. Whether Jesus is *in, under, with, around, or all up in* the elements, I don't know, but I have come to understand that God is present and zealous for us in that meal. It should be approached with the utmost gravity and the highest joy. As a younger man, I was often so bound up with guilt and shame that I frequently avoided communion for fear of what I had been taught regarding 1 Corinthians. In some sense, I felt the need to have had perfect behavior before I could take communion, to make myself worthy of the Eucharist, and I missed the point entirely! It is Jesus who is worthy. It is Jesus who is host of the meal. He is the One serving the elements. Do you want him? Run to him! All your desire is there in the breast of the Father, in the presence of Son and Spirit. In that meal, we partake in the very nature and intention of God. This is where our shame and guilt-based preaching has done such terrible damage. The Pharisees would have us try to be perfect on our own merits, so we can approach God. But God would have us run to him as we are, and he will deliver us from our sin. So yes, we are persuaded of the terror of the Lord, but we also know that it is the goodness of God that leads us to repentance. See 2 Cor 5:11, Rom 2:4.

As we pan out from this myopic, the heart of God is revealed even more. Matthew 9:10-13 records the occasion of Jesus eating at Matthew the tax collector's house. Then, more tax collectors and "sinners" started showing up, much to the consternation of the religious rulers. The old joke goes that Jesus ate with sinners because there was no one else to eat with. But, there is a very strong point in this: we are *all* concluded together in a common lot as sinners. See Rom 3:23,

The Agape Feast

Gal 3:28, Rom 11:32. God's verdict is the great equalizer of all humanity.

I will quote Brennan Manning at some length here:

> "Jesus extended grace to sinners by sharing meals with them. It has a much deeper meaning than we in our culture ascribe to it. It is an offer of relationship. It is impossible to overestimate the impact these meals must have had upon the poor and the sinners. By accepting them as friends and equals, Jesus had taken away their shame, humiliation, and guilt. They mattered. Physical contact. Through table fellowship, Jesus ritually acted out His insight into Abba's indiscriminate love-a love that causes his sun to shine upon the bad men as well as the good."[1]

When I read Jesus' commendation of the church in Ephesus, (Rev 2) I am struck by the quality and the quantity of work they are doing. They are diligent, patient, and faithful. They are guarding the spiritual gate. They have endured trials. It is obvious that Jesus is proud of them. I certainly am! There's a church doing legitimate work. They are holding the line for God. They are laboring in faith for his name's sake. Then Jesus drops a bomb on them. Even in their faithful, sincere striving, they have lost sight of their true object of worship. These were good-hearted, kingdom-minded people. I have wrestled with this passage, wondering if Jesus wasn't being a bit unfair, a bit harsh. These folks are working for his name's sake! They have suffered. They have endured. I could but aspire to this level of Godly commitment. But Jesus knows what is at stake, the loss of relationship with him, the loss of their light in this world as work takes over relationship. Even suffering is not the metric.

A Christian Ethic for the Modern Church

1 Corinthians 13 tells us that love, *Agape*, is the metric. Jesus knows that "in all things he must have the preeminence" (Col 1:18, KJV). He knows where this is headed, even when we have the best intentions.

In verse five Jesus counsels us to "Remember therefore from where you have fallen; repent, and do the works you did at first. If not, I will come to you and remove your lampstand from its place, unless you repent" (Rev 2:5). While there may be much conjecture and many scholarly ideas on what constitutes "first works," I believe it involves the very things we have been discussing in this section, the life of the early church in Acts, the woman in the gospels who broke precious ointment on the feet of Jesus, Mary sitting at his feet and hearing his word, the cessation of labor for labor's sake, the spirit of the Eucharist, the sharing of meals and this world's goods, sharing the circle of life in committed, organic relationship. It means the end of religious pretense.

I have not said much about orthodoxy, right doctrine, or what we might call spiritual formation, and that is by design. These things are without a doubt crucial. There is a dire need in our society for defined truth, for objective reality, for some port in this storm! Balmer and Winner noted, "The most successful religious movements in America have been *exclusive* and not inclusive, [that] evangelicalism ... offered certainty-a clearly articulated theology and morality in an age of moral ambiguity ..."[2] The gospel message is still Jesus Christ crucified. It is still the call to repentance and holiness. The Bible. The Creeds. The Church universal. The problem for us in this area is that in pursuit of orthodoxy and religious observance, we have so often left the living person of Jesus, of God himself, and the human beings whom we are charged to love that we might check all the right boxes. We are not even speaking the same language oftentimes. What we call ministry is often means and methods. What does God call pure religion? "Religion that is pure and undefiled before God the Father is this: to visit orphans and widows in their affliction, and to keep oneself unstained from the world" (James 1:27). What we call orthodoxy has often taken the place of the living and revealed God in Jesus Christ, and our religious observances have obscured his transcendent reality *a la* Barth in *On Religion*. Revelation 21:3 expresses succinctly all that we have been discussing. It is the desire, the intention, and the purpose of God. It is the expression of his love, fellowship, and inalienable nature, and that which we should seek to emulate as children in his service, "And I heard a great voice out of heaven saying, 'Behold, the tabernacle of God is with men, and he will dwell with them, and they shall be his people, and God himself shall be with them, and be their God'" Amen.

AFTERWORD

This work represents my reflections on over forty years of church experience along with several years of intensive reading and study. The church in America is, in my opinion, at a crisis point. Numerous cultural and historical factors, our current pandemic included, have coalesced to bring us to a unique opportunity and imperative. The Church in America must change if she hopes to recover the kind of influence that I think God intends. We must repair ourselves from the damage done by the inappropriate use of money, power, and politics.

When I began attending the home church several years ago, and teaching ESL, I had no idea the impact it was going to have on me. I finally felt like we were doing church as it was intended. I was reminded of all those glimpses I'd had in the past, the meals, the time spent, the relationships, the giving.

Currently, we are reading through the Bible front to back, and discussing it. We have coffee. We let the kids run amok for a few before they go to their lesson. We talk about life. We pray. Then we eat lunch together. We sometimes have lengthy and heated discussions about differences in our beliefs, and then we seek reconciliation and understanding. We grow from it. We get together other times to help people, to have coffee and talk, or to have holiday parties. Our overhead is just the cost of making lunch, which we rotate. We know that there will be challenges, but I still would not trade our experience.

Our host family has had the ESL students over for meals and parties before. We have formed relationships with all sorts of international folks, and sometimes we can help them with their needs. We help each other frequently.

We have attended a local gathering of Persian Christians a couple of times now. The worship and preaching are in Farsi, but we are finding a relationship and the fellowship of God's spirit. We are sharing meals. We are learning something from a group of Christians who have different priorities than we do in their lives and prayers. Some of the people who come do not even believe in Jesus yet. I believe this is as it should be.

It caused untold guilt, fear, and shame and a very long time to leave the institution and visit our home church, but I can now say that I feel like I am truly engaged with a body of folks that mirrors what we see in Acts. I am not suggesting that this is the answer for everyone, but I will suggest that a deep work of renewal is urgent in our time.

As for this writing, I apologize with deep sorrow if I have misrepresented anyone, or if I have gotten any facts wrong. I apologize for not recognizing with sufficient force the untold good so many Americans have done and are doing for the world, for the tragedy of unwilling complicity, and the difficulties that historical realities so often unfairly cause sincere people. I apologize if my tone has been harsh. Nothing could be further from my desire, even though I must be honest about my anger and hurt. I am angry at the state of our world. I am often angry at God because I do not understand why

Afterword

he allows the depths of senseless human cruelty. I am angry at him and us for the brokenness of his Church. I desire to see the Church renewed in simplicity, community, humility, healing, and hope. As I did my research and reading, and as I recounted my own experience, I began to see how desperate is our need, and how urgent is the imperative for us to change.

Some of the points I did not develop at length because they have been written about extensively, and expertly, by others, and I do not have the resources at present to commit to a massive work. I was also suffering a significant illness that ended my firefighting career while I wrote this work. I trust that the recommended reading list will be helpful.

As for the spoon I mentioned in the introduction, I'm pretty sure I sold it in my antique booth. Maybe it will find better use at the shared table.

I hope and pray that you will find the heart of God, the community of the saints, and a place of revolutionary being in the kingdom of God.

ACKNOWLEDGMENTS

Mandi, Clara, and Anna thank you for being such a wonderful family. Mandi, thank you for your love, support, and belief, and for listening to the rough drafts. Thank you for your many prayers.

I would like to thank Becky Haigler for her invaluable support in proofreading, editing, criticism, and validation. You went above and beyond the call of duty!

Thank you to Josh Wood and Co. for reading and critiquing, and for being such a hospitable home-church for us. You guys are an example for us all.

Thanks to Dan Bush for being a friend throughout my career as a first responder, for being a Christian brother, and for your financial gift to help with publishing. Thanks to your family as well, for always being kind to me.

Thank you to all the folks at Roasters Coffee and Tea Co. in Amarillo for your kindness, coffee, and for letting me park my butt for the last twenty years.

Thank you to Darryl Birkenfeld of Ogallala Commons for listening, taking me seriously, and modeling holism and community.

Thank you to Silent Hands Deaf Chapel, to David, Cindy,

Jason, Jerry, Linda, Robert, and others who loved and accepted us.

Thank you to the Amarillo Fire Department for teaching me so much, through good times and hard times, and for providing a living for our family.

Thank you to the ESL ministries at Paramount Baptist Church, and the Refugee Language Project who helped build bridges across pain and anger to a new level of understanding. You also connected me with Trauma Healing Institute, which is helping provide a new direction in my life.

Thanks to Jerika Balfour for the cover design.

Thank you to the several strangers who met me in the coffee shop, and promised to pray for me and this little book.

Thank you to Cathy Burns, Christin Hall, Rynn Burkett, Monique Arritt, and mothers and sisters who have helped walk me through healing.

Thank you to Martin Luther, Henry Thoreau, Henry Nouwen, Francis Schaeffer, Brennan Manning, and others whose depth, suffering, and willingness to better the human condition have sustained me through many dark nights of the soul. You are fathers I wish I could have met in person, and whom I hope to emulate.

10
NOTES

On the Kingdom of God

1. Eugene McCarraher, *The Enchantments of Mammon: How Capitalism Became the Religion of Modernity* (Cambridge: Belknap Press: an imprint of Harvard University Press, 2019), 300.

2. John W DeGruchy (quoting Slane), *Bonhoeffer's Questions: a lifechanging conversation* (Lanham: Lexington Books/- Fortress Academic), 56.

3. DeGruchy, 142.

4. Martin Luther King, Jr, *Why We Can't Wait* (Lees Summit, MO: Beacon Press, 2011), 34.

5. NT Wright, *Surprised by Hope: Rethinking Heaven, the Resurrection, and the Mission of the Church* (New York: HarperOne, 2008), 245.

Prayer

1. Randall Balmer, *Thy Kingdom Come: how the religious right distorts the faith and threatens America, an Evangelical's Lament* (New York: Basic Books, 2006), 189.

2. NT Wright, 193.
3. Ibid. 199.

On the Christian in the World

1. Arlene Hirschfelder, *Native Amerians: a history in pictures* (New York: Dorley Kindersley Publishing, Inc, 2000), 8.
2. Derrick Jensen, *The Culture of Make Believe* (White River Junction, VT: Chelsea Green Publishing Co., 2004), 11.
3. Ibid. 160.
4. Martin Luther King, Jr, 96.
5. Ibid. 98.
6. DeGruchy, 10.
7. Jacques Ellul, *The Presence of the Kingdom* (Colorado Springs: Helmers and Howard, 1989), *xli,* from introduction by Daniel Clendenin.
8. McCarraher, 289.
9. Dorothy Sayers, *Letters to a Diminished Church: passionate arguments for the relevance of Christian Doctrine* (Nashville: W Publishing Group, 2004), 90.
10. James Howard Kunstler, *Living in the Long Emergency: global crisis, the failure of the futurists and the early adapters who are showing us the way forward* (Dallas: BenBella Books Inc., 2020), 209.
11. https://www.statista.com/statistics/196104/total-are a-of-land-in-farms-in-the-us-since-2000, accessed 10/19/2020
12. Wright, 232.
13. Greg Glassman, Founder of Crossfit, *Fitness in 100 Words.*
14. Brennan Manning, *The Ragamuffin Gospel: good news for the bedraggled, beat up, and burnt out* (Multnomah, 2005), 57.

Notes

Creation Care and Stewardship

1. Laura Walls, *Henry David Thoreau: a life* (Chicago: University of Chicago Press, 2017), 438.
2. Ibid. 186
3. deGruchy, 56.
4. Mike Magee, *Code Blue: inside America's medical industrial complex* (New York: Atlantic Monthly Press, 2019), 4.
5. Kunstler, 171.
6. https://www.neighbor.com/storage-blog/self-storage-industry-statistics/ accessed 10/22/2020

Christianity, the Political Apparatus, and the Media

1. Francis Schaeffer, *How Should We Then Live: the rise and decline of Western thought and culture* (Wheaton IL: Crossway Books, 2005), 19-20.
2. Ellul, 87.
3. https://www.statista.com/statistics/257337/total-lobbying-spending-in-the-us/ accessed 10/23/2020
4. Kunstler, 243.

On the Institution of Church in America

1. Randall Balmer and Laura F Winner, *Protestantism in America* (New York: Columbia University Press, 2002), 214-5.
2. Ibid.
3. Manning, *Ragamuffin*, 103.
4. https://www.christianpost.com/news/12-megachurch-salary-tithing-and-mission-trends-report.html accessed 10/30/2020

A Christian Ethic for the Modern Church

A Proposed Organizational Ethic Drawn from Several Sources

1. Ellul, 124.
2. Ibid. 77
3. *Twelve Steps and Twelve Traditions* (New York: Alcoholics Anonymous World Services, 1986), 9-10.
4. Walls, 186.
5. Jensen, 160.
6. Kunstle,r 212.
7. Jensen, 99.
8. Ellul, 97.

A Proposed Personal Ethic Drawn from Several Sources

1. Viktor Frankl, *Man's Search for Meaning* (Boston: Beacon Press, 2006), 36.
2. Schaeffer, 180.
3. Manning, 13.
4. Ellul, 105, 97.
5. Manning, 110.

The Agape Feast

1. Brennan Manning, *Abba's Child: the cry of the heart for intimate belonging* (Colorado Springs: Navpress, 2015), 61.
2. Balmer and Winner, 195.

11
RECOMMENDED READING

This first group of books is about God, the love of God, and spiritual development. I would recommend them heartily:

Surprised by Hope, NT Wright, outstanding work about the gospel, and how it impacts us, our world, our activism, and our eternity. A wonderful exposition of a holistic gospel.

Celebration of Discipline, Richard Foster, classic and compassionate work on the spiritual disciplines.

The Ragamuffin Gospel, and *Abba's Child*, by Brennan Manning, I spent a long time with these books. I gave away many copies. They are excellent expositions of the love of God for broken humanity.

Soul Survivor, Philip Yancey, A great book that restores hope to those who have been disillusioned by church, and even Christianity. It is an analysis of several Christian people who have lived exemplary lives of faith. See his book on Prayer as well.

True Spirituality, Francis Schaeffer, This short book is a great primer for the spiritual life. It helped me get rid of some unrealistic expectations, but also helped me see that substantial healing is available in every facet of the Christian's life.

A Christian Ethic for the Modern Church

Knowing God, JI Packer, classic about who God is, and what the gospel is.

These next two books are about the organic life of fellowship and emphasize meal sharing and home churches:

The Gospel Comes with a House Key, Rosaria Butterfield, This is a great book on the blessing and imperative of Christian hospitality.

Letters to the Church, Francis Chan, the last half is my favorite, as the author talks about how they do home church.

These are two great books about the importance of creation care to the gospel:

Creation Care and the Gospel, Colin Bell and Robert S White, eds.

Creation Care: A Biblical Theology of the Natural World, Douglas J Moo, and Jonathan A Moo

Next:

For the Life of the World, Toward a Social Ethos of the Orthodox Church, https://www.goarch.org/social-ethos, I discovered that I am not alone by any means in my concerns. This is a fairly comprehensive document compiled by a team of educated theologians and members of the Orthodox Church, addressing the issues of our time.

Walden, Henry David Thoreau, This is a classic work that opened my eyes to new ways of thinking about the world. It is a profound meditation on simplicity, spiritual connection with life and others, the proper ordering of one's life and commodities, and the *opposite* of the utilitarian construct we live in. It is still a timely work. While Mr. Thoreau has often been criticized regarding the nature of his "experiment," an honest reading will yield powerful insights into our modern psychology, and hopefully clear up common misunderstandings about his purposes in building and inhabiting the cabin at Walden.

Recommended Reading

The Nature Principle, Richard Louv. This book and others by Mr. Louv explain the surprising depth of nature's importance to human beings across a staggering array of domains including crime and community development, climate, mental and physical health, education, economics, and more.

Twelve Steps and Twelve Traditions, This is an exposition on the concepts behind the twelve-step program Alcoholics Anonymous. The value of it for our purposes is in its traditions, which are the hard-won truths that have allowed their fellowship to survive at the group level. The issues they faced and overcame are universal to any group of people who wish to build community. A great study.

This next group is important social and psychological criticism:

The Presence of the Kingdom, Jacques Ellul, An introduction to his philosophy and criticism of our utilitarian society and the need for Christian understanding.

The Culture of Make Believe, Derrick Jensen, A six hundred-page meditation on the manifestations and psychology of hatred in Western society. This is a deeply disturbing book, but it illustrates just how endemic hatred, objectification, and utilitarianism are in our society, and how deeply rooted hatred is in our psyche.

The Enchantments of Mammon, Eugene McCarraher, A massive and extensively researched work outlining the development of a dehumanizing industrial America, and the complicity of the Protestant church. This is painful, but important work.

Thy Kingdom Come, Randall Balmer, This is a work exclusively criticizing the "Religious Right," and outlines how a subset of conservative Christians have often responded to historical setbacks by taking misguided and damaging political action, and the injuries it has caused to our witness. A very enlightening read for me. Takes a critical look at a lot of individuals and organizations that many conservatives might consider the vanguard of the faith.

A Christian Ethic for the Modern Church

Why We Can't Wait, Dr. Martin Luther King Jr, This is an eloquent exposition on the psychology of the civil rights movement of the 1960s. It is an excellent primer for the right kind of Christian activism, and it also exposes some of the less helpful thinking that exists out there.

I am not Your Negro, Raoul Peck, James Baldwin.

On the Duty of Civil Disobedience, Henry David Thoreau, A convicting classic, and a short read; this one should be essential for all of us.

Lies My Teacher Told Me, James W Loewen, A book that explores historical revisionism in school textbooks. An enlightening read.

World War II: the rest of the story and how it affects you today, 1930 to September 11, 2001, Richard Maybury. Confronts many deeply held beliefs about the history of American warfare and propaganda. Will be an uncomfortable read for many, but is exemplary of the type of psychological work the West needs to undertake.

Live Not by Lies, Rod Dreher, Encapsulates ideas presented in *The Origins of Totalitarianism,* and *The Gulag Archipelago,* with emphasis on the development of harmful ideologies, and how Western Christians may be faced with increased hardships moving forward. It draws on the experiences of those Christians who endured Soviet communism and who are now seeing disturbing and familiar patterns emerging in the West.

Sword of the Spirit, Shield of Faith: Religion in American War and Diplomacy, Andrew Preston.

The Vegetarian Myth, Lierre Keith, An enlightening book about the ravages of industrial agriculture, and its deeper implications of it for the broader society. This one has a lot more information than I provided, from someone who knows the subject matter. I do not agree with all of her conclusions, but the book is devastating and necessary nonetheless, and I respect her work.

Recommended Reading

The Lubbock Disparity Report is an analysis of the race, class, and economic elements the author found unsettling in the development of his community. It showed how wealth was extracted from older neighborhoods to fund the building of new developments to the detriment of infrastructure in a sort of Ponzi scheme, how districts were divided along racial lines to force minorities into certain schools, how the location of industrial operations in poor neighborhoods perpetuates poverty and racism, etc. One local example of the destruction of myth perhaps.

https://firstuulubbock.org/wp-content/uploads/2020/06/Lubbock-Disparity-Report.pdf

Countdown, Alan Weisman, a look at the impact of human presence, behavior, and population on the earth and society. Contains many psychological insights including the benefits of human symbiosis with nature and the overwhelming benefit and need for female education, especially in developing nations.

Ecclesiastes 12:12 states, ". . . of making many books there is no end, and much study is a weariness of the flesh."

In light of that truth, I understand that this reading list and this entire work may be naive and limited by many standards. Maybe it is just something I needed to do. Maybe I am wrong about many things I have asserted, but there is much work to do and we have to start somewhere.

The Scripture continues, "Let us hear the conclusion of the matter: Fear God, and keep his commandments: for this is the whole duty of man. For God shall bring every work into judgment, with every secret thing, whether it be good, or whether it be evil (Ecc 12:13-14).

www.ingramcontent.com/pod-product-compliance
Lightning Source LLC
Chambersburg PA
CBHW060513090426
42735CB00011B/2201